AND ONE PILL
MAKES YOU SMALL

AND ONE PILL
MAKES YOU SMALL

Overcoming Fear With Facts and Faith

Randy Crenshaw, MD

RESOURCE *Publications* • Eugene, Oregon

AND ONE PILL MAKES YOU SMALL
Overcoming Fear With Facts and Faith

Resource Publications
An Imprint of Wipf and Stock Publishers
199 W. 8th Ave., Suite 3
Eugene, OR 97401

www.wipfandstock.com

ISBN 13: 978-1-4982-2505-2

05/26/2015

Contents

Acknowledgments

I owe a debt of thanks to many people for their help in making this book come to life. The constant encouragement of my literary friend, Proal Heartwell, caused me to stick with this work after I had given it up for dead. I am grateful for his friendship. Mike Richardson inspired me to begin putting information together in my head years ago, when he introduced me to The Dartmouth Atlas of Health Care. His inspiration has reached full bloom now. Ken Wilson, performing the work of copyeditor, made the book more readable through his considerable skills.

Introduction

Broken promises litter the landscape of the American dream. Our doctors and scientists told us they held the secrets that would enable us to find significance, security, and satisfaction. They claimed that changing our brain chemistry would make us content and confident—happy and fulfilled. They alleged that eating right and exercising would bring us peace of mind and long life. They declared that taking drugs which interfere with nature's exquisitely designed physiologic systems would prevent heart attacks and strokes—and prolong our lives.

This is the morning after for American medicine. We have awakened to find that promises made in the heat of commercial passion look much less certain in the blinding light of day. A new class of drugs to combat depression works only one-third of the time—the same rate as *placebos*. Diets and weight loss programs, on average, succeed even less often. Pharmaceuticals that block the body's natural production of cholesterol rarely prevent vascular catastrophes; they also cause diabetes and memory loss in a significant number of patients.

Medical care used to be a very personal and humanistic interaction between a doctor and a patient. Now medical offices work more like assembly lines. Instead of compassion they dispense fear. Patients have little say in which tests and treatments are ordered. To add insult to injury, much of what is ordered does not improve the health status of the recipients.

Introduction

This book is my attempt, after forty years in the medical trenches, to help you distinguish science from sales hype—to separate the wheat from the chaff. I hope to soothe your fears by giving you facts you can use and by building up your faith. After you've read it, I am confident you'll be able to face doctors who spend their days prescribing medicines that don't work to people who can't afford them. God has not given his people a spirit of fear, but of power and wisdom. We're the body of Christ! We have the mind of Christ.

Chapter 1 addresses back pain, one of the most common reasons for visits to doctors. Despite a lack of evidence proving its superior efficacy, major surgery to fuse the vertebrae has exploded in popularity. Other therapies for back problems produce results as good as surgery and carry much less risk.

Chapter 2 explores the myths around the causes and cures for depression. It examines the outcomes of talking therapy and of drug therapy, and it assesses the risks involved in using potent psychoactive substances to make people feel better about their lives.

Chapter 3 inserts *hope* in what appears to be a losing situation. Even though many of the drugs and devices on the market do little to assuage human suffering, all is not lost. The Bible contains "prescriptions" for most of life's ailments through its unique perspective on human nature. This chapter serves up helpful reminders of God's never ending affection for his people—in their creation, redemption, preservation, and glorification.

Chapter 4 examines the results of efforts to prevent broken bones by using drugs that block one of the body's natural aging processes. These drugs are fraught with risks, and they are not very effective at preventing hip or wrist fractures. The fear of deformity in the spine from softening or thinning of the vertebrae is being blown out of proportion. When it does occur, it is not usually painful.

Chapter 5 looks in detail at the "war" on cholesterol being waged by the the federal government and its allies, Big Pharma. The production of cholesterol by our bodies serves several important purposes, including one by the brain. Interfering with that process by taking statin drugs causes impairment of memory in some people. In about two percent of users it causes *diabetes*. Contrary to popular belief, statins *do not prolong life* when taken by people to prevent heart disease. The death rate is the same for those who take them as it is for those who don't.

Chapter 6 evaluates the economic impact of medical care on individuals, families, and nations. Americans now spend 2.7 trillion dollars—over 17 percent of the nation's GDP—on medical care each year. Much of that world record spending has little or no impact on the health and longevity of the people. I'll show how variations in medical practice from one region of the country to another contribute to this gross waste of resources.

Monopoly privileges granted to doctors, hospitals, insurance companies, and drug makers make price-lowering competition all but impossible. Uneven treatment in the income tax code gives substantial advantages to people who have employer-sponsored insurance. States have passed laws requiring insurance plans to cover certain services, many of which consumers do not use and do not want to buy. I'll describe an alternative system that over-comes the disadvantages inherent in the current system—one that puts the patient in charge.

Chapter 7 appraises the options available to us at the end of life. People who live in certain regions of the United States are more than twice as likely to die a *high-tech death* in a hospital than Americans living in other areas. New York has the the highest rate of in-hospital death (41 percent), and Utah has the lowest (16 per-cent). In spite of the fact that more than 80 percent of surveyed patients say they wish to avoid hospitalization and intensive care during the terminal phase of illness—and they write living wills to avoid such torture—hospitals routinely ignore them and press full speed ahead.

You don't have to take chemotherapy on the last day of life! I will show you a better way of preparing for your departure to Heaven.

CHAPTER 1

By The Sweat of Your Face

Cursed is the ground because of you;
in pain you shall eat of it all the days of your life.

GENESIS 3:17

I believe the first backache occurred in the Garden of Eden. When they failed to follow their maker's instructions, God pronounced a curse on the man and the woman. He told Adam that he would have to labor and toil on a relatively unproductive ground to get food to eat. Because the human race spread out, back pain now covers the face of the whole Earth.

In my experience most cases get better in a couple of weeks without any treatment at all. In spite of that, billions of dollars are spent each year on doctor's visits, diagnostic tests, and various remedies for neck and back pain. According to WebMD, low back pain is one of the most common reasons for visits to the doctor. In a survey, one in four adults reported having low back pain in the last three months.

Over the last decade CAT scans and MRIs have become increasingly common in the diagnosis of spinal disorders. Narcotic prescriptions, injections around the vertebra, and surgery have exploded in popularity. Most of the money spent on these supposed cures is wasted. Researchers at of the University of Washington reported in the Journal of the American Medical Association that patients did not get better results, just higher costs.

Some things haven't changed much in the last 2000 years. The New Testament records an encounter between Jesus and a woman with persistent, unrelenting, uterine bleeding. Mark 5:25–30 says that she'd been bleeding for twelve years, and she "had suffered much under many physicians, and had spent all that she had, and was no better but rather grew worse." Those of you with chronic, recurring back or neck pain can identify.

BMJ Clinical Evidence, a publication of the British Medical Journal, is one of my "go to" places to find the best information about the effectiveness of the most popular and common therapies. Their researchers perform systematic reviews of the clinical trials published in the English language. In their review of acute low back pain (pain present less than twelve weeks) published on their website on May 9, 2011, they say

- NSAIDs (ibuprofen family) and muscle relaxants improve symptoms, but they sometimes cause adverse effects. Trade offs are involved.

- There are no studies on the effectiveness of steroid injections in acute low back pain.

- It is not known whether spinal manipulation (chiropractic), acupuncture, back schools, behavioral therapy, massage, multidisciplinary treatment programs, lumbar supports, TENS, temperature treatments, or exercises make any difference in acute low back pain.

The medical evidence leads to the conclusion that this painful condition is usually *self-limiting*. That's doctor-speak for "it gets better with no treatment." I'm not saying it's all in your head, but the times I have personally come down with disabling back pain were times of high stress in my life. The chapter on depression adds more to this overly simplistic and utterly unhelpful statement, so don't close the book yet.

Chronic Low Back Pain (published 08 Oct 2010)

On the same website I discovered that about 75 percent of people in developed countries develop low back pain at some time, and their symptoms usually improve in less than two weeks. A small number of patients, however, have symptoms persisting after one year of follow-up care. The percentage of patients who describe their back pain as "chronic" has increased, from less than 5 percent in 1992 to more than 10 percent in 2006. In the highest-quality, randomized, controlled clinical trials (the "gold standard" in medical research) BMJ Clinical Evidence makes the following observations about the effectiveness of a variety of medical, physical, psychological and surgical therapies.

- NSAIDs might be more effective than placebos.

- Narcotics might improve pain and function compared to placebos, but they have well-recognized adverse effects.

- We don't know whether antidepressants reduce pain or improve function more than placebos. Suicidal behavior might occur more often in those who use antidepressants.

- Benzodiazepines might lessen pain.

- We don't know if steroid injections improve chronic low back pain in people without sciatica (pain running down into the leg).

- Spinal fusion is no better than intensive rehabilitation with a cognitive behavioral component. (This again raises the question of the role life's stresses play in causing back pain. The chapter on depression sheds more light on this.)

- Acupuncture, back schools, and chiropractic manipulation may reduce pain in the short term, but their effects on function are unclear.

- Massage may lessen pain and improve function.
- We don't know whether biofeedback, lumbar supports, traction, or TENS provide pain relief.
- We also don't know whether electrothermal disc therapy or disc replacement lessens pain or improves function. Ditto for radio frequency destruction of the nerves.

Variations in Medical Practice

The science then, sadly, is insufficient to steer us toward a satisfactory solution to the ubiquitous problem of lower back pain. This uncertainty, no doubt, explains a curious phenomenon uncovered by the researchers at Dartmouth University. There is no "standard" way of treating back pain in the United States, or of treating many other conditions for that matter. On January 29, 2015 I went to their really good website (dartmouthatlas.org) to look afresh at the section called VARIATION IN THE CARE OF SURGICAL CONDITIONS. There they describe the problems:

> "For many conditions, surgery is one of several care options, and in some instances, there are several types of surgical procedures available. Research into the effectiveness and adverse effects of a surgical procedure compared to alternatives is often incomplete. While quality has generally improved over time, outcomes can differ across hospitals and surgeons. Too often, treatment options, whether medical or surgical, are recommended without patients fully understanding the choices and participating in the decision; and these recommendations can vary markedly from one physician to the next."

Looking specifically at spinal fusion, I uncovered some observations that are hard to explain, given the fact that fusions have *not* been shown—in the best studies done to date—to give people better results than less-risky, non-surgical treatment. Bear with me as I shift into nerd mode to give you some idea of the scope of the problem.

- The rate of spinal fusion operations for lumbar spinal stenosis among Medicare beneficiaries age sixty-five and over increased 67 percent between 2001 and 2011.

- The average rate among regions in the U. S. during that period was forty-one per one hundred thousand, but the rate varied wildly and dramatically across the three hundred and six hospital referral regions. Bangor, Maine Medicare patients had nine procedures per one hundred thousand while Medicare patients in Bradenton, Florida had one hundred and twenty-seven. Stated another way, if you live in Bradenton you are fourteen times more likely to receive fusion as a treatment than if you live in Bangor! Here is a break down of the five highest and five lowest use regions in the U. S.

Bradenton, FL	127.5
Grand Rapids, MI	89.9
Mason City, IA	89.2
Tyler, TX	88.5
Newport News, VA	87.4
Bronx, NY	17.5
Scranton, PA	17.1
Alameda County, CA	14.9
Fresno, CA	12.5
Bangor, ME	9.2

Spinal surgery in general is highest in the northwestern United States. Washington, Oregon, Idaho, Montana, and Wyoming have surgery rates far in excess of the rest of the country. When I was a resident in orthopedic surgery in one of those states, it was my job to do a history and physical exam on all the patients admitted to the hospital by surgeons in private practice. Late one night as I wearily approached the door of my next "work up," I faced a woman who was scheduled to get some injections in her lower back the next day. When I saw the scar on her lumbar spine, I asked her how long ago she had been having surgery. She answered with a smirk, "Which time? I've had twenty-two operations on my back!" The fact that she had done more than her share of the training of young orthopedists in her forty two-years on earth did not seem to comfort her.

Those of you who disdain uncertainty will be dismayed to discover that spinal surgery is *not* the exception to the rule. In the fifteen years I've been analyzing these data, I've come across several common surgical treatments whose rates vary widely from one city to the next. Knee replacement, coronary stents or bypass, and prostate cancer surgery—just to name a few—are also all over the map.

Some of you have very personal experience with this phenomenon. All surgical operations carry a risk of complications and adverse results. Compared to simple *decompression* procedures for back pain, complex fusions are associated with greater risks of life-threatening complications and death. The Dartmouth data shows the probability of such serious complications to be three times greater with fusion than with decompression. Readmission to the hospital occurred 8 percent of the time in the latter, but in the former the rate was 13 percent. For all types of spinal surgery taken together, the two-year rate of repeat operation was 17 percent, and 25 percent were readmitted to the hospital for a complication resulting from surgery.

How in the world can medical practice be so different in cities that are sometimes just a few miles from each other? Are all the doctors in Bradenton crooks? Are they getting financial kickbacks from the makers of the devices they implant in your body? Probably not. Because of the often poor state of clinical science, surgeons recommend surgery on the basis of subjective opinion, personal experience, anecdote, or untested clinical theory that might prove to be false when subjected to some actual science.

Another problem lies in the way medical decisions are made in America. The extreme variations I describe above arise because patients commonly expect their doctor to make the decision about treatment for them. Yet studies show patients often choose different treatments when they are fully informed about their options.

This state of affairs will not likely change until patients are routinely engaged in shared decision making that takes into account their
personal preferences. Only then can they make truly informed
choices about what treatment is best for *them*.

An environment of that sort would have helped my patient,
Donna. She injured her knee in college athletics, and a surgeon
took out the cartilage separating the thigh bone from the lower leg
bone. (The formal name for her operation is meniscectomy.) Years
later she developed arthritis not only in that knee but in the opposite knee as well. After years of suffering with constant pain in both
knees she consulted another orthopedic surgeon. He advised her
to have her knee joints "cleaned out," because the arthritis inflam-
matory process had created a lot of debris—loose cartilaginous
stuff that was clogging up and preventing full movement of the
joint.

He also mentioned that her kneecaps appeared to be "off center," and he wanted to move them into a more normal alignment.
I knew from my own surgical training that he was advising the
treatment currently in vogue with knee surgeons, so I thought it
might actually help her with the pain and lack of motion in both
knees. She had the worst knee fixed first, and she was so sick after
the anesthesia that she had to be admitted to the hospital for ob-
servation overnight.

She had the same operation on her other knee a year or two
later, with the same result—she threw up like crazy after the anesthesia wore off. The physical therapy ordered by the surgeon was
extremely painful, and she suffered through that to find she could
not walk all that much better after surgery. For a few years the pain
was less than before, but the range of motion of the knee joints was
about the same as before surgery.

A few years later, I found an article in a medical journal that
caught my attention. A bright young orthopedic surgery resident
at a Texas hospital could not understand why cleaning out the
knee joints of people with arthritis would give them less pain and
more movement. He devised a perfectly simple clinical trial to see
if this standard procedure was effective, or was just the *placebo*

effect at work. With patients who agreed to participate in the trial, he performed the standard operation on every other one. In the other half, the control group, the patients got a *sham* surgery.

The standard operation comprised a small incision over the knee joint through which a new tool, the arthroscope, was inserted into the joint space. Copious amounts of water flowed into the joint out of bottles hung from a pole, while a suction device drained the water out. All the patients had spinal anesthesia so they could be awake during the procedure. The control group, which received the sham operation, had the same set-up. This time, however, the surgeon made the small incision but did not insert the arthroscope into the joint. He ran the water and the suction device, not into the joint, but into the superficial incision he had made. To the patients, it appeared they were getting the real procedure. The results of his trial showed *no difference* in pain or function a year later in the treatment group compared to the control group.

CHAPTER 2

The Stress of Not Getting What I Want

"Why are you cast down, O my soul?"

PSALM 42:5

Call me skeptical. After long years of looking at the evidence—I really don't remember when I started this search—I do not believe a chemical imbalance in the brain causes us to feel depressed, dispirited, dejected, unhappy, miserable or gloomy. I know this opinion puts me outside the "mainstream" of thought in medical circles in 2015, but the weight of the evidence just doesn't support this theory. Some brand name scientists, however, agree with me; it's an interesting theory but not yet fully formed fact.

Problems With The Biochemical Theory

My conclusion is based on a few facts and observations I've collected from a variety of sources.

- While two things (a depressed mood and altered levels of certain chemicals in the brain fluid) may occur together, the one didn't necessarily *cause* the other. Chemical changes could be the *effect* of depression. Or a third thing, like stress, could have caused both of them to appear at the same time.

- In studies comparing different treatments of depressed people, talking therapy worked just as well as drugs designed to combat a supposed chemical imbalance.

- The Prozac (fluoxetine) molecule is eerily similar to the chemical structure of methamphetamine (aka, "speed"). Fluoxetine is chemically (*RS*)-*N*-methyl-3-phenyl-3-[4-(trifluoromethyl)phenoxy]propan-1-amine. Speed lacks only the three fluoride ions present in Prozac.

- Many people with depressed moods get better spontaneously, without any treatment or professional attention.

- We all feel sorrow and sadness at times. Who decides when those emotions are not appropriate? On the contrary, I worry about people who are not profoundly sad at living in a world at war with the God who created and sustains it.

- Some people have *melancholic* personalities and show a life-long tendency toward sadness.

- Me? I have a *choleric* temperament, so I tend toward anger. You can see it in photos of me when I was young. (A couple of years ago I found my medical school graduation photo in a box of stuff. There I was, walking across the stage, diploma in hand, looking resplendent in my cap and gown. My future was bright, and it should have been the happiest day of my life. As I studied the snapshot forty years later, I wondered, why was I so angry? It looked like I was ready to kill, not to heal!) How long will it be before Pfizer or Merck brings to market a pill to control anger? Then we can call it a disease, and insurance will pay for my prescriptions.

Aside from these concerns, it troubles me that the pharmaceutical companies have been deceptive. What do I mean? Just that they never published in medical journals the results of many clinical trials they performed to get FDA approval of these antidepressants. Under the Freedom of Information Act some journalists recently got the unpublished studies. Sharon Begley of Newsweek reported that the "concealed" studies were those in which the drug didn't work! The drug makers submitted forty-seven studies during the approval process. Forty percent of them were not published for the medical professionals. Practicing physicians saw only the favorable studies. Taking all the studies together, half of them showed no difference in the drug and the placebo. The other half showed a very small improvement in the patients who got the real drug.

A recent article in the Journal of the American Medical Association admitted as much. Vanderbilt University researcher Steven Hollon, PhD commented that "the very small" benefit of antidepressant drugs compared to the dummy pills "is what my colleagues call 'our dirty little secret.'" He concluded that "most people don't need an active drug." The authors of the article found the active drug had only a two-point advantage over the dummy pill in a fifty-four-point depression questionnaire.

Are you surprised that just taking a *placebo*, an inert pill with no active ingredient, makes some people feel better? (The word placebo in Latin is translated "I will please.") Doctors have always known that one-third of their patients will get better if they just try *something*. It appears the Jefferson Airplane has it right in its raucous, riotous, Sixties cult favorite song, White Rabbit. She laments that the pills her mother gives her don't do anything at all.

What then? If prescriptions don't work for most depressed patients, as current television ads admit, what can we do when sadness overwhelms us? On April 21, 2010 and again on January 10, 2015, the BMJ Clinical Evidence website rates two types of psychotherapy as "Beneficial" in depressed patients. Here are their definitions:

> Cognitive Therapy: Brief (twenty sessions over twelve–sixteen weeks) structured treatment aimed at changing the dysfunctional beliefs and negative automatic

thoughts that characterize depressive disorders. It requires a highly trained therapist.

Interpersonal Psychotherapy: Standardized form of individual brief psychotherapy (usually twelve–sixteen weekly sessions) primarily intended for outpatients with unipolar depressive disorders without psychotic features. It focuses on improving the person's interpersonal functioning and identifying the problems associated with the onset of the depressive episode.

Professional assistance, then, whether medical or faith-based, does help us feel better according to the best scientific studies. Many people of faith, though, consider counseling to be "psychobabble" (and some of it really is). So for years I've looked for clues in the Scriptures to get a better understanding of the problems people encounter in a broken world and of the solutions endorsed by the author of Scripture, God the Holy Spirit.

Romans 12

Chapter 12 in Paul's letter to the Roman church gives one of the best treatments of this subject I've found so far. Here's the entire chapter, but check out verse two especially.

> 12:1 I appeal to you therefore, brothers and sisters, by the mercies of God, to present your bodies as a living sacrifice, holy and acceptable to God, which is your spiritual worship, your rational service. 2 Do not be conformed to this world, but be transformed by the renewal of your mind, that by testing you may discern what is the good and acceptable and perfect will of God.
>
> 3 For by the grace given to me I say to everyone among you not to think of himself more highly than he ought to think, but to think with sober judgment, each according to the measure of faith that God has assigned. 4 For as in one body we have many parts, and the parts do not all have the same function, 5 so we, though many, are one body in Christ, and individually members one of another. 6 Having gifts that differ according to the grace

given to us, let us use them: if prophecy, in proportion to our faith; 7 if service, in our serving; the one who teaches, in his teaching; 8 the one who exhorts, in his exhortation; the one who contributes, in generosity; the one who leads, with zeal; the one who does acts of mercy, with cheerfulness.

9 Let love be genuine. Abhor what is evil; hold fast to what is good. 10 Love one another with brotherly affection. Outdo one another in showing honor. 11 Do not be slothful in zeal, be fervent in spirit, serve the Lord. 12 Rejoice in hope, be patient in tribulation, be constant in prayer. 13 Contribute to the needs of the saints and seek to show hospitality.

14 Bless those who persecute you; bless and do not curse them. 15 Rejoice with those who rejoice, weep with those who weep. 16 Live in harmony with one another. Do not be haughty, but associate with the lowly. Never be wise in your own sight. 17 Repay no one evil for evil, but give thought to do what is honorable in the sight of all. 18 If possible, so far as it depends on you, live peaceably with all. 19 Beloved, never avenge yourselves, but leave it to the wrath of God, for it is written, "Vengeance is mine, I will repay, says the Lord." 20 To the contrary, "if your enemy is hungry, feed him; if he is thirsty, give him something to drink; for by so doing you will heap burning coals on his head." 21 Do not be overcome by evil, but overcome evil with good.

Look again at the definition above for cognitive therapy. It fits Romans 12:2 like a glove! When Paul says, "Be transformed by the renewal of your mind," what else does he mean than to change dysfunctional beliefs and negative automatic thoughts? The *world* holds up one pattern for us to imitate, and the *Word* holds up another, entirely different one. This letter encourages the Christians at Rome to recognize and reject the pattern of thinking, feeling, and behaving they see all around them in people who do not have faith. Instead, it says, embrace the will of God if you want to really live! Beginning at verse nine, the apostle gives us some concrete examples. We change our dysfunctional beliefs by substituting these precepts (and others found scattered throughout the Bible) for the things the world values. By now you're probably thinking that this is easier said than done. Let's break it down.

Offering ourselves wholly to God to use as he pleases holds no appeal whatsoever to our human nature. We don't trust him to provide the kind of life we think we need, so we go off in search of a route to happiness that *we* ourselves map out . He knows we're doing this, so he eventually sends the Holy Spirit to live in each one of his adopted sons and daughters. The Spirit gives us *the desire* to serve the Lord, and that's a very big deal. He also teaches us to trust God (and on most days we feel that we can). After following the Spirit for a while, we learn to discern what's good and what's not. But the Lord sometimes withholds from us things we feel we can't live without. Argh-h-h-h! This is not as easy as we'd hoped it would be. On some days it feels like death.

Now he shows us some more stuff about ourselves that repulses us. The Bible calls this *repentance*. It's not the soul-searing feeling of worthlessness we wear when somebody judges us—but a heartfelt *sadness* that leads to refreshment after we see that we're wrong about something or someone. We're not as wise as we thought we were; we begin to *doubt* ourselves. We are really sorry for the hurt we've caused other people; we don't know how to fix it. But your secular doctor just says you're depressed and wants you to try this drug. Do you see where this is leading?

Hopefully we begin to see how *merciful* the Lord has been in his dealings with us. Suddenly, it seems only logical to devote ourselves to *his* program, not our own. After all, he rescued us from a lonely, miserable life of self-interest and self-deception; he adopted us into his family; he made us a part of the body of Christ on earth. He then equipped us to serve a particular role in that body, and some of us discovered for the first time what we're really good at.

No longer believing that we don't need other people, we are eager to associate with like-minded friends. Our attitude about people changes too. Not content now to love them superficially, or to use them, we genuinely desire good for them. No more fake love, no pretense. We are just as concerned about their welfare as our own, and we make sacrifices for them we never dreamed we would make.

Old acquaintances begin to notice we've changed. They no longer see our bitter jealousy, our fiery anger, our stony stubbornness, or our disabling anxiety. One of my high school girlfriends even noticed it over the telephone! She had gotten divorced and wanted to know if I was available. In the middle of the conversation she injected, "You don't sound like yourself." On another occasion a grumpy physician working with me in the emergency room asked, "How come you're always so happy?"

Then we begin to see ourselves doing the really hard things. The love, the joy, the peace, the kindness and gentleness oozing from the pores of our souls occasionally grates on the nerves of those who don't have it. They labor behind the scenes to undermine us. Or they publicly ridicule and revile us. Having humbled ourselves under the hand of God, we decide not to satisfy ourselves by retaliating, and we pray that the Lord will show them a better way. If the opportunity arises, we even do tangible acts of kindness toward them!

Psalm 42–43

The Bible doesn't confine itself to Romans 12 in giving us help for such a prevalent and pressing affliction. The Psalms paint vivid portraits of suffering, shame, adversity and affliction . . . and the Lord's deliverance from them. Jesus' human ancestor, David, the second king of Israel, wrote many of these Hebrew poems. Samuel records the highlights of the life of David in his second book. In one of the darkest hours of his legendary life, King David contends with one of his sons, the ambitious Absalom, who craves the throne for himself (2 Samuel 14–18).

Absalom begins his plot by killing his stepbrother, Amnon, the first-born son of David. (The immediate cause of this fratricide is Amnon's rape of Absalom's sister, Tamar. David, like many of us, is no stranger to sexual intrigue. The prophet Nathan tells David trouble will come on his kingdom because he took Bathsheba, the wife of another man, to be his own.)

After stealing the hearts of the people of Israel, this handsome scoundrel lays out to the leaders his plan to take the throne from his father. When he hears of it, David and those closest to him depart the city on foot in chaos. In an especially poignant scene, it says that "David went up the Mount of Olives, weeping as he went, barefoot and with his head covered."

We believe David penned Psalm 42–43 (it might have been all one psalm in the Hebrew Bible) to express the agony, the absolute despair he felt on that occasion. Its universal appeal rests on the fact that sadness, panic, and fear are tightly woven into the fabric of life on a planet under the curse of its Creator (Genesis 3). All of us, being honest with ourselves, will acknowledge that we're acquainted with this sort of grief.

Notice how David pours out his lament to God, then he gives himself a "pep talk" to dispel the doubts assailing him. He reminds himself specifically how God delivered him in the past; how the Lord rescued him out of deep water; how he provided food, family, and friends when David was on the run and his life seemed beyond repair, when it seemed certain his enemies would win, when loss and failure loomed large.

Can you remember times when God liberated you? When disaster seemed imminent, but your heavenly Father came through for you in a way you never dreamed of? When I think back, many such "rescues" come to mind! The grief might last too long, in our opinion, but it will come to an end. God will send relief and make everything beautiful in his time. Meanwhile we share in the sufferings of Christ, and God disciplines all his adopted sons and daughters.

Should I Quit Taking My Antidepressants?

A few years ago some researchers in behavioral medicine came up with a brilliant idea. They would enroll test subjects from two groups of patients—those who had been receiving only "talking therapy" (cognitive therapy or psychotherapy) and those who were taking only "drug therapy." To the patients in each group, they then added the other therapy—the one they had not yet tried. In other words, those who had taken only drug treatments added psychotherapy, and vice versa. In a totally unexpected and remarkable finding, at the end of the treatment period the patients who added psychotherapy to their former regimen of drug treatments got clinical improvement. On the contrary, the patients who were in talking therapy got no better by adding prescription drug treatments.

In the end, only you can decide what treatment to take. Your mother can't make the decision for you (unless you're a minor); your pastor cannot; and neither can your physician. You have the mind of Christ, and the wisdom that comes from above is pure and open to reason.

However, parents, professionals, and close friends are valuable resources, and "without counsel plans fail, but with many advisers they succeed" (Proverbs 15:22). A social support system makes dealing with depression manageable. Hang out with other committed Christians who have the knack for encouragement. (Avoid the Bible Bullies!) Adopt a new way of thinking about the pressures of *time*.

We can't control the events of life, but we can recognize that there is as much good as bad coming around. The patriarch Job asks the right question when he suffers unbearable tragedy—should I accept prosperity from the hand of God and not also adversity? There is an order to human life, and we can plug into the flow of time. King David's son Solomon writes that:

> "For everything there is a season, and a time for every matter under heaven:
>
> a time to be born, and a time to die;
> a time to plant, and a time to pluck up what is planted;
>
> a time to kill, and a time to heal;
> a time to break down, and a time to build up;

a time to weep, and a time to laugh;
a time to mourn, and a time to dance;

a time to cast away stones, and a time to gather stones together;
a time to embrace, and a time to refrain from embracing;

a time to seek, and a time to lose;
a time to keep, and a time to cast away;

a time to tear, and a time to sew;
a time to keep silence, and a time to speak;

a time to love, and a time to hate;
a time for war, and a time for peace."

He concludes with words that have lifted me up more than once from the depths of despair and depression: "he has made everything beautiful in its time. Also he has put eternity into man's heart . . . I perceived that there is nothing better for them than to be joyful and to do good as long as they live; also that everyone should eat and drink and take pleasure in all his toil—this is God's gift to man" (Ecclesiastes 3:1–13).

There may be a time to take drugs and a time to give them up—but we never have to give up hope. We have the promises of God made sure in Jesus Christ, who serves now in Heaven as our great high priest. "For we do not have a high priest who is unable to sympathize with our weaknesses, but one who in every respect has been tempted as we are, yet without sin. Let us then with confidence draw near to the throne of grace, that we may receive mercy and find grace to help in time of need" (Hebrews 4:15–16).

CHAPTER 3

Our Days Are Numbered

In your book were written, every one of them,
the days that were formed for me.

Psalm 139:16

Long before our mothers gave birth to us, the sovereign King of Heaven and Earth determined how long we would live. Writing through Israel's King David, the Holy Spirit eloquently describes our human situation in Psalm 139. Beginning with single cells in our mothers' wombs, God fashions and frames us. As the cells multiply he weaves them together. He forms all two hundred and six bones that hold us together and make us stand up on two feet. He separates our specialized tissues into organ systems and gives them their unique functions. Then he records on a scroll in the heavenly register of events exactly how many days we will live on the earth (Psalm 139:16).

Because he creates us, God knows us inside and out. Sometimes I wonder who in the world I am, but he does not wonder. He knows everything about me. He knows my thoughts, even what I am going to say before I say it. He understands my moods, my ups and downs, and he is not amazed or dismayed that I myself do not understand them. He even determined that I would work as a physician during my relatively brief time here on earth.

Though God created man and woman to live forever, because of their disobedience he cut short their days. By the time the Israelites wandered forty years through a vast and dreadful desert, God had determined the span of human life would be seventy or eighty years. Psalm 90:10, thought to be a prayer of Moses, adds, "yet their pride is but toil and trouble."

If you look at United Nations or CIA life expectancy tables of the industrialized nations of the world, you will see that Japan ranks first at eighty-two years and Turkey last with seventy-two. At the turn of the century in 1900, before we had discovered antibiotics and vaccines, a seven-year-old boy in the USA lived on average to age sixty-five. Our experience seems to mirror that of the Israelites 1400 years before Christ descended to earth to dwell among us. The Bible claims to be (and I believe it to be) the revelation of God the Creator to his creatures about himself and about ourselves. It is not a scientific treatise, but what it says about the life span of humankind matches what science currently measures and teaches.

Jesus the Healer

Some people think medical science can extend life way past a hundred years. Personally I'm putting my money on Indiana Jones finding the Ark of the Covenant *and* the crystal skull before that happens. Many people I talk with believe they can forget about dying if they can just get enough good medical care. Neither the Bible nor the scientific evidence supports such a notion.

Some common misconceptions are running rampant in the medical marketplace. How many times have you heard that you have to get screened for cancer so doctors can catch it early? Screening saves lives, we're constantly being told. The reality? People who get regular screenings for breast or colon cancer die of *something* at the same rate as those who don't go for check ups, mammograms, and colonoscopies. (When you look at deaths caused specifically by breast or colon cancer, the death rate is microscopically lower in those who get screened year after year. One person in 2000 is helped by screening; the other 1999 get no benefit at all. It is duplicitous to say that life is *prolonged* by screening.)

In some cardiology practices, the same deceptive sales techniques are used. No lives are saved when people who *don't have heart disease* take drugs to lower their levels of cholesterol; neither does coronary artery stenting save anyone's life. Stents help to relieve pain from sluggish blood flow to the heart muscle, but they don't prolong life.

Trinitarian belief says God exists as three persons: The Father, The Son and The Holy Spirit. I assume most of you are trinitarian, but I'm sensitive to the fact that some of you who read this are not. In his letter to the Colossians, the Apostle Paul writes in chapter 1:16 that "all things were created by Christ and for Christ." The (unknown) writer of the New Testament letter to the Hebrews says in chapter 1: 2 that "Christ made everything and *upholds it* by the word of his power." It makes perfect sense that mankind's fall from grace concerns Jesus. His beloved disciple, John, said that the reason Jesus came to earth was to reverse the effects of the Fall. In his own words, "For this purpose the Son of God was manifested, that he might destroy the works of the devil" (1 John 3:8).

The first book of the Bible supplies the account of the disobedience of Adam and Eve in the Garden of Eden (Genesis 3:15). God promises them that one of the offspring of the woman will crush the head of the serpent, who embodies Satan at that moment. (Christ's death and resurrection will fulfill that promise.) The promise doesn't mean humans will not die; it simply assures the first humans that God will provide a remedy for the mistake they made.

Jesus repeatedly demonstrates his concern for his people during his earthly ministry. In the fifth chapter of his gospel, Mark describes an instance of miraculous healing performed by the Master. One of the officers in the Jewish church, Jairus, pleads with Jesus to come to his house and heal his terminally ill daughter.

A huge crowd presses in on them as they walk along, and delays them a good while. As they go on their way, someone comes up to them and says the girl is dead. Put yourself in this man's shoes. The news takes your breath away! Then you hear someone in the crowd coarsely complain that they needn't bother Jesus any more about it.

Jesus ignores them and takes her parents and three of his disciples into the house. They go into her bedroom and find her truly dead. Jesus grasps her hand and commands, "Little girl, get up!" The twelve year old stands up and walks around the house. Astonishing!

Faith Healers

Some Christians today think that God routinely heals by miraculous power, and they avoid going to doctors for help when they're sick. After all, the Bible has little to say about physicians, and most of what it does say is not nice. Perhaps they know people who've had bad experiences in the health care system, and they don't want to risk that. Some believers trust in modern medicine, but they choose to go to hospitals known for faith healing. They've seen it happen on television and they think, "That could work for me."

Others who shun the health care system reckon that God has numbered their days, so why worry about their health. *Que sera, sera.* Whatever will be, will be. Perhaps those who choose not to vaccinate their children fall into this category.

On the other hand there are Christians who take the opposite approach. They read in the New Testament that our bodies are temples of the Holy Spirit; therefore they believe they ought to avail themselves of the best modern medicine has to offer. They figure God allowed us to discover these miracle cures, and we need to do our part in staying healthy. Which group has it right?

Striking a Balance

In my capacity as Executive Medical Director of a WebMD company, I served six years on the medical advisory board of an independent software firm. During one of our meetings we were having a heated discussion. One of the other physicians, a good friend, shouted at me, "You wouldn't take any treatments!" Over the years I had so often quoted the evidence showing how ineffective many popular treatments are, they concluded I must be a Christian Scientist or something worse. I assure you nothing could be further from my real opinion.

After I finished my first year of training in surgery, the federal government sent us to the Dakotas to work in a hospital for the Sioux. When we arrived they gave me a routine physical exam. On my chest X-ray appeared a suspicious spot in the upper part of the right lung. My skin test for tuberculosis raised a huge whelp on my arm, and the CDC sent an infectious disease specialist to look me over. He concluded the spot on my lung was an active TB infection and he prescribed two medications for me to take for two years.

In the nineteenth century England of Charles Dickens and George McDonald, tuberculosis was a sentence of death. I praise God that we had antibiotics by the time I got infected. Talk about religion—I didn't miss a single dose in two years! My colleague on the medical advisory board was wrong. I will take some treatments, but I pick my battles. The ability to fight infectious diseases marks a milestone in modern medical science. Antibacterial and antiviral drugs undoubtedly reduce suffering and prolong life. In the same way, advances in trauma surgery have saved people who would have perished in previous generations.

I remember very well one patient who especially proved this point. Carrying her baby in her arms, a mother ran frantically into the ER through the sliding glass doorway used by ambulance drivers. Pleading for us to help her, we reassured her and took her eighteen-month-old daughter from her. As I held the almost lifeless child, I noticed her head did not move when I put my hand under it. Her neck was so stiff it didn't flex, and I knew right away she had meningitis. My exceptionally competent nurse, Lee, started an IV, then held the baby while I did a spinal tap. The appearance of the fluid would tell the tale. Normal spinal fluid looks like water. In bacterial meningitis it looks like something you'd squeeze out of a pimple. Fortunately, I found the fluid-containing space in the lower spine on the first needle puncture. The thick, white fluid came out under enormous pressure and we had our diagnosis. I phoned the academic medical center across the street and asked the senior resident in pediatrics which antibiotic to start infusing before we transferred her to their specialized care. The child and her happy mother eventually left the hospital and she made a full recovery. Fifty years ago she would have died that day.

Shalom

When the Bible talks about health it commonly uses the Hebrew word "shalom." In other passages that same Hebrew word is translated "peace," "prosperity," "satisfaction," or "contentment." Is this not simply the one thing we all long for? When the Rolling Stones complain that they can't get no satisfaction, we all feel their pain.

In writing the New Testament, the human authors of Scripture used the Greek language. Through the inspiration of the Holy Spirit, they often use the same word for "heal" as they use for "save." God is our health *and* salvation, and the Bible makes no distinction between the two. So why do we Christians go to secular doctors just as much, or more, than unbelievers do?

Two primary factors, in my opinion, account for this phenomenon. On the one hand, it is very easy to get medical care in America. In the late 1980s the Congress passed a law requiring all hospitals receiving Medicare payments (and they all do) to treat every person who shows up in the ER, regardless of their ability to pay the bill. Because our insurance system makes it financially painless to get medical care when we need it, our market system creates an abundance of willing providers of care. These purveyors swamp us with information and advertisements that make it seem not only desirable to get treatments but foolish to abstain. To put it succinctly, we have a lot of capacity in our health care system.

On the other hand, we have a dire shortage of the knowledge of Biblical Christianity. This combination is causing some serious repercussions! So this seems like a good time to remind ourselves what the Scriptures teach about health and healing. After all, God gives the Scriptures to us "to make us wise for salvation through faith in Christ Jesus" (2 Timothy 3:15).

Faith

After Adam and Eve fall from their state of innocence in Paradise (Genesis 3), death and disease become the norm for humanity. In today's parlance, it is the *default* position. Let's call this position "unbelief." Our first parents do not believe God's promise—that he will give them unending bliss if they obey his instructions.

Unbelief lives in the heart. Not the anatomical heart through which your doctor threads catheters and wires, but the part of us we call the spirit, or the soul. God determines early on that he will heal this unbelief with an antidote called faith. So we say, "I believe, Lord; help my unbelief!"

In his introduction to his lectures on Romans, Martin Luther, the Protestant reformer of the sixteenth century, has this to say about faith.

> "Faith is a living, daring confidence in God's grace, so sure and certain that a man would stake his life on it a thousand times. This confidence in God's grace and knowledge of it makes men glad and bold and happy in dealing with God and all his creatures; and this is the work of the Holy Ghost in faith. Hence a man is ready and glad, without compulsion, to do good to everyone, to serve everyone, to suffer everything, in love and praise to God, who has shown him this grace" (Mueller's 1954 translation).

Circulating in the churches today is the idea that people can make themselves believe simply by willpower. The Bible describes it differently—that faith is a *divine* work in us. It changes us by causing us to be born anew as "children of God, who were born, not of blood nor of the will of the flesh nor of the will of man, but of God" (John 1:13).

In Genesis 4:3–7a we see faith at work in the first human family. Adam and Eve conceive two sons, Cain and Abel. The Bible text says "In the course of time Cain brought to the lord an offering of the fruit of the ground, and Abel also brought of the firstborn of his flock and of their fat portions. And the lord had regard for Abel and his offering, but for Cain and his offering he had no regard. So Cain was very angry, and his face fell. The lord said to Cain, 'Why are you angry, and why has your face fallen? If you do well, will you not be accepted?'"

Implicit in this passage is that God gives some instruction about offerings, and Cain fails to follow them. The New Testament often explains and clarifies cloudy parts of the Old. Hebrews 11:4 says that Abel's offering is better because it springs from faith. God views Abel as righteous because God gives him faith, plants it deep in his heart.

The Heart Transplant

The prophet Ezekiel describes this process as a heart transplant. He says in Ezekiel 36:26–27:

> "And I will give you a new heart, and a new spirit I will put within in you. And I will remove the heart of stone from your flesh and give you a heart of flesh. And I will put my Spirit within you, and cause you to walk in my statutes and be careful to obey my rules."

God gave me a new heart in August of 1977. Through the ministry of my precious wife and of an author named Catherine Marshall, he made me a new person. Years later I wrote down what I understood to have happened on that hot summer night.

> We hurtle past the milestones—runnin' late.
>
> The ladder of success seems no great height

when power, pleasure, riches so delight

the senses raw, feed flesh, intoxicate.

Ignore the clatter. Rush and rant and rave—

distracted by the skirt that clings skintight.

Stiff-neck booze mitigates at day's twilight,

then we awake to find desire enslaves.

The hunger deep inside, though, goes unfilled

until, unnoticed, Love arrives to free

us from our selfishness—the plague that kills.

Now to the Son of God I bend the knee.

To serve suffuses with a quiet thrill

the vibrant heart made new by grace decreed.

In the language of the church we say I was saved. I was also healed. I was no longer compelled to practice those things that were hurting my body and my mind.

The Bondage of the Will

Those of us lucky enough to be born and raised in America are mostly convinced we're in control of our world. I see now I was not in control. I was doing things that were messing up my life, but I couldn't quit doing them. Through many hard trials I learned what the Bible means when it says, "you are either slaves to sin or slaves to righteousness" (Romans 6:18). God gave Martin Luther, an obscure Roman Catholic priest in Germany, profound insight into these mysteries and launched, in 1517, a revolution in religion that changed the course of world history. Luther wrote "The Bondage of the Will" to help his congregation understand the concept of slavery to sin. I admit the language is a little archaic, but he did a masterful job of explaining a core principle of Christianity. If you're not game for that, at least buy his commentaries on Galatians and Romans. They explain Biblical Christianity (which is losing ground fast) as well as anything I've read in nearly forty years of studying.

In a workshop I attended for pastors and teachers, the English minister John Stott said that he hoped we would learn to view Christianity as a religion of *rescue*. He was standing on solid ground there. In a letter to his disciple Timothy, the apostle Paul instructs him to correct his opponents with gentleness, because "God may perhaps grant them repentance leading to a knowledge of the truth, and they may come to their senses and escape from the snare of the devil, after being captured by him to do his will" (2 Timothy 2:25–26). Captivity is not a notion that fits well into modern society. Someone will say, "it certainly feels like I'm free to do what I choose." In one sense they would be right. We are free to rearrange our furniture and throw out the trash, but not so free to get rid of our anger, our stubbornness, our lust, or our fears.

Christian psychologist Larry Crabb portrays the effect of the rebellion in the garden of Eden as leaving all of us with a deeply rooted determination to find a route to happiness we can control. In corporate America the secret dream of many is to become an independent contractor; sports heroes long to be free agents. But spiritually speaking, there are no free agents. The Bible makes it clear we are either slaves to sin or slaves to righteousness.

Unless God gives us a new heart, we are chained to unhealthy lifestyles. We cannot control ourselves until the Holy Spirit comes to live in us and produce self-control. No drug can overcome "addictions" like smoking or drinking too much. (We ignore the real recovery success rates—about 10 percent—and reckon we just need more willpower to go with the drugs.) If we are prone to eat too much, we go get an acid blocker to make us comfortable again.

Now I myself am not skinny. If you've seen me you know I do not despise food. We went to Tuscany a few years ago, and the aromas of that place are indelibly etched on our brains. We even try to copy the recipes in our kitchen at home! Do I feel guilty? Not for a minute. The Bible says there is nothing better on earth than being happy and eating and drinking and enjoying our work

(Ecclesiastes 5). Sign me up! So a large part of health consists in serving God with gladness and undivided loyalty.

Redemption Through The Death of Christ

The Bible also depicts our rescue from disease and destruction as *redemption*. By dying on the cross, Jesus secures our release from Satan's domain. His heavenly father adopts us as sons and daughters. Jesus is the only *begotten* son; the rest of us are his brothers and sisters by adoption. God loves us just as he loves the birth son. He delights in us, and we are under his care and protection. We are not perfect yet, but the perfect life Jesus lived on earth is credited to our account. When the righteous judge of all the earth looks at us, the verdict is "*not guilty!*"

When Abraham was really old and still childless, it is said of him that he believed God would provide an heir, and this is *credited* to him as righteousness (Genesis 15:6). Knowing God will provide for us, we can live healthy and happy lives in the household of faith. We can live *contented* lives, not worrying about what we will eat or drink or wear. Or where our next paycheck will come from. Or how our children will turn out.

Another aspect is peace, and it shares a close connection with contentment, or the satisfaction we feel with God's plan for our lives. I remember the months just before I was born by the Spirit of God. My life was not going in the direction I had planned and I was not at all happy about it. I decided to have a talk with my minister. We met several times and I thought we were getting nowhere. Out of frustration during one of these sessions, I blurted out "I just want to find some peace!" I believe that every heart that hungers for something more than this world has to offer utters that plea at one time or another.

Jesus tells his disciples, in the last long talk he had with them, that his parting gift to them is peace (John 14). He bequeaths to them a sense of confident satisfaction that the world knows nothing about. Not the flimsy sort of peace that comes from closing a big deal or winning election to high public office (now that I think about it, those are roughly equivalent), but a peace that accepts a cancer diagnosis with tranquility. A calmness that says, "God is in control" when you are on your way to bail your son out of jail. An aplomb that takes a pink slip in stride.

Paul writes to the Philippians (and to us) to remind us to worry about nothing. He tells us to pack all our concerns in prayer and ship them to God, who will supply us with a serenity we simply cannot wrap our minds around (Philippians 4:7).

This peace is Jesus' to give, because he paid for it with his life. On the cross at Calvary he voluntarily surrenders his life so his people can live. (It occurred to me recently that God also saved his people in the old covenant through a wooden instrument—Noah's ark—when he destroyed the entire human race minus eight.)

Jesus makes peace with his heavenly Father for us in that one act of atonement. Since the first man—one of only two human beings in all of history with completely free will—decides to make a go of it independent of his Creator, all of his descendants are under the sentence of death. In his great mercy, God sends his son to serve as a substitute for us. After living the perfect life we could not live, Jesus takes on himself the punishment prescribed for us. "By his wounds you have been healed" (1 Peter 2).

Some Christians have interpreted that statement to mean we should never be sick. I have actually heard church people say, "You would get well if you had more faith." I probably said it myself as a young believer. Peter's letter simply does not lend itself to that conclusion. Christians do suffer sickness, and sometimes our heavenly Father uses bodily illness to bring us home to himself.

When Passion Turns to Pain

I've heard that Francis Bacon said the reward for obedience in the old covenant was wealth and prosperity, but in the new covenant the reward is suffering. C.S. Lewis called pain God's megaphone to rouse a deaf world. If things are as good between God and us as I've painted them, why then do we suffer? Does suffering serve any useful purpose?

Our Days Are Numbered

A few years ago a runaway best seller bore the title, "Why Do Bad Things Happen to Good People?" In his book Rabbi Kuschner explores the universally perceived injustices we see in the news and in our neighbors' lives almost every day. We all know people who work hard at helping others bear their burdens, who volunteer to lend a hand when tragedy strikes, who are the first to reach out sympathetically to comfort and console those whom life has dealt a serious blow. Then we learn that someone who is constantly sacrificing for others has come down with cancer or lost a son or daughter in a car wreck. We simply cannot make sense of it. We rage against the universe and ask ourselves if God could not have prevented this catastrophe. Sometimes it makes us feel like life is meaningless.

The American philosopher John Stuart Mill wrestled with this question in the earliest days of our nation's birth. He settled his inquiry in this way: God cannot be all powerful *and* all good. If he allows evil to cast a shadow over our joy in life, he is not the benevolent deity we imagine him to be. If he sees evil happening and cannot stop it, he is not omnipotent.

In Genesis 18:25, Abraham, the Old Testament hero called Father of the Faithful, dares to ask God to his face, "Shall not the Judge of all the earth do what is just?" (God has come down to Abraham and revealed to him his plan to destroy Sodom and Gomorrah.) Abraham simply cannot believe God would destroy the good people along with the bad. In his distress, he launches a series of negotiations with the Almighty! God assures Abraham he would not destroy the cities if he could find ten righteous people in them.

It's All Good

In the New Testament the Apostle Paul spends a lot of time on the question, "Why do bad things happen to Christians?" His conclusion will shock some of you. *They don't!* Saying that, I don't mean in any way to trivialize the troubles you're facing right now. I myself once told a colleague who watched me suffering through an excruciating business failure that it was making me doubt the goodness of God.

So what does Paul mean when he writes that God uses all the bad stuff for our ultimate good (Romans 8:28)? He's not saying evil isn't present in the world—some really awful things are going down in the lives of people he dearly loved. He just means to say that God *causes* it all to work together for good for those who love him, even when it all feels hopeless. Not even the devil can frustrate the sovereign purposes of God Almighty.

The opposite theological error is also rampant today. Friends sometimes tell me that God has nothing to do with suffering. Whenever I hear that, it infuriates me. God has everything to do with suffering! Bible teacher R.C. Sproul says, "God majors in suffering! He redeems his people through suffering. To say he has nothing to do with our worst moments takes all hope away from us." Because Jesus suffered, his followers will suffer; but God will triumph *through* our suffering.

Several years ago I read Dr. Sproul's book "Surprised By Suffering." The chapter title "Suffering As a Vocation" captured my attention. At some time in every Christian life, the call ("vocation" in Latin) of God is to suffer. Pain and suffering does not come to us by *chance*. Can you imagine anything worse than thinking life works that way? No; if we know God has a purpose in it we can endure it.

How Does God Do It?

I referred earlier to Martin Luther's commentary on Romans. His insight into this problem as it is addressed in Romans 5 is worth the price of the book all by itself. Here is how Luther explains it. Tribulation works patience in us. (Remember that in our fallen state we are not by nature patient. We want what we want when we want it.) God shapes us in the fire of affliction so we can see whether we're using him or really delighting in him. In other words, do we love God for his own sake and not just to get what we want? The fire takes away everything important to us and leaves us naked and destitute. It causes us to despair of ever finding happiness apart from this Father who loves us. It drives us to seek help and solace from him alone.

The Christian can interpret suffering not as angry judgement—God is punishing me—but as loving discipline designed by our heavenly Father to train us in perseverance. It cures us of insisting on having our own way. We can find joy in trials because they give us the confidence, the assurance, that we will one day see him. When that day comes, our joy will be inexpressible. On that day he will wipe away every tear from our eyes. There will be no more suffering—no agonizing cancer, no heartbreak, no dementia.

Until then we cling to this hope, we wander as aliens and exiles on the earth, on our way to a better home (1 Peter 2). We stay alert since we might leave this world at any time (Second Corinthians 5). We purify ourselves so we'll be like Jesus when he stands to welcome us to the place he has prepared for us in Heaven (1 John 3).

CHAPTER 4

Brittle Bones: a Bonanza for Big Pharma

This at last is bone of my bones

Adam—Genesis 2:23

Mrs. Olsen is a tall, thin, attractive woman with grey-white hair and a dignified demeanor. She has worked as a court reporter for forty of her sixty-four years, and she is proud that she quit smoking a few years ago. She says it was the hardest thing she's ever done. She's looking forward to retirement next year after spending so much of her active life in "the dungeon," as she likes to call the court room. Her children are grown with families of their own now, and she and her husband want to travel and see the world.

She went to see an endocrinologist recently, after her primary physician had diagnosed osteoporosis on a bone density scan. The Fosamax he prescribed is upsetting her stomach, but she doesn't want to stop taking the medicine for fear of another fracture. Five years ago, she broke her wrist when she fell ice skating. The bone surgeon had recommended calcium and vitamin D supplements from the health food store. Apparently that hadn't kept her bones

healthy and strong. Gripped by uncertainty, she sought professional advice.

Mrs. Olsen's story is typical of millions of post-menopausal
women in the United States. The ads they see on television every
evening worry them. Could I be the next to break a hip? Will I
have to go into a nursing home? Will I end up with that hump on
my back, bent over like my mother? Scary stuff. Fortunately, the
grim picture painted by the drug companies materializes less often
than imagined.

Big Business is Not Your Friend

On January 21, 2000, the Washington Post published a letter written by aging actress Debbie Reynolds to advice columnist Ann
Landers. Ms. Reynolds urges all post-menopausal women to talk
to their doctors about getting tested for osteoporosis. She adds, "If
you test for it early enough, you need not get osteoporosis in the
first place. It absolutely can be prevented."

Debbie was really cute in her 1950s movies "Give a Girl a
Break" and "The Tender Trap," but she fell into a trap when she
wandered off into a field owned by big business. It turns out, according to Emory's Professor Davis, that she was a "paid spokes-
person for an initiative funded by Merck, which manufactures the
top-selling osteoporosis drug, Fosamax." Merck's strategy? To get
as many women as possible tested, so they would become patients
given a diagnosis of osteopenia or osteoporosis. Portable machines
measuring bone density sprang up in doctors' offices all across
America, and the number of prescriptions for Fosamax surged.

Ms. Reynolds is quite mistaken if she believes osteoporosis
can be prevented. Fosamax does increase bone density in some
women who take it, but it does not prevent very many fractures.
I'll delve into the details shortly.

A few years ago I read a book by Fox News legal analyst, Judge
Andrew Napolitano. I do not remember the name of the judge's
book, but I'll always remember one statement he made: "Big business and big government are not your friends."

This he culled from decades of experience on the bench in New Jersey. It is, possibly, the most profound thing I have learned (speaking as a citizen of the world) in the new millennium. Many years earlier, the iconoclastic American song writer Bob Dylan had come to the same conclusion. In his song Tombstone Blues, Mr. Dylan was more colorful than the judge, likening Jack the Ripper to the head of the Chamber of Commerrccce!

Iconoclast might be a new word to you. Here's the definition offered by my Apple Mac:

> iconoclast (noun)
>
> 1 a person who attacks cherished beliefs or institutions.
>
> 2 a destroyer of images used in religious worship, in particular
>
> > • historical: a supporter of the eighth- and ninth-century movement in the Byzantine Church that sought to abolish the veneration of icons and other religious images.
> >
> > • historical: a Puritan of the sixteenth or seventeenth century.

Since we're talking about "clasts" at this moment, it's probably a good time to provide a refresher course on bone physiology. Osteoclasts are the cells that break down bone in our bodies. (Osteoblasts are the ones that build up bone.) Both cells are working at the same time, but one cell type dominates the scene early in life when we are building new bone and growing; the other dominates at the end of life when we are winding things down. Osteoclasts are regulated by several hormones, including PTH from the parathyroid gland, calcitonin from the thyroid gland, and growth factor interleukin.

Osteopenia, Osteoporosis, and Fractures

The drugs known as biphosphonates, for example Fosamax, Actonel, and Reclast, exert their influence by blocking the natural action of the osteoclasts. The theory? In some women the osteoclasts "overdo it" and the bones become thin or "brittle." We say that women who have lost some bone "density" in bone scans (compared to younger women) have osteopenia. Those who have lost more have osteoporosis.

Smoking tobacco appears to increase the chances a woman will develop osteoporosis. So does being thin and Caucasian. Finally, it does run in families. Women whose mothers had osteoporosis are more likely to have it.

Such fragile bones break slightly more often than those that are not so brittle, but the differences are not dramatic. You can see this in the data from randomized controlled trials of three specific drugs promoted to prevent fractures. I choose these three, because they are the only drugs proven conclusively to reduce the odds that a woman will suffer a fracture of all the bones we usually think of as osteoporotic fractures: the vertebrae (spine or backbone), the wrist, and the hip. Some of the other drugs prescribed for osteoporosis will decrease the chances of breaking one or another of those bones, but these three appear to exert an effect in protecting all three types of fractures. Two are available in oral form and one requires injections.

In a minute I'll create a table that compares the effectiveness and the risks of Fosamax, Reclast and Actonel. Some preparatory remarks are in order first, because the subject is a little complex.

Before I went to med school, I thought of a fracture as a clean break in one of the long bones of the body, like an arm or a leg. When I studied orthopedic surgery I learned about another variety called "compression" fractures. These often occur in the back bone, that is, the vertebrae of the thoracic and lumbar spine. Sometimes a fall or a car wreck will cause compression of a vertebra when the back is bent suddenly forward.

When you X-ray women over fifty years of age you sometimes see similar compression deformities. They do not happen suddenly in an accident, but over the years as the bones soften due to age and the other risk factors mentioned above, these vertebrae lose some of their height in the front part of the bone. They rarely hurt or cause pain. They never, in my experience, cause paralysis or problems with the spinal cord.

I mention this because the scientific papers on fracture prevention in osteoporosis divide fractures into two categories: vertebral and, well, non-vertebral. (This is one way you can tell doctors are not marketeers. They would have invented a clever name for the latter type of fractures.) Occasionally these vertebral compression fractures do cause symptoms, but more often than not we find them as a coincidence. If several of them undergo this gradual compression, however, it can cause a permanent deformity. You've probably heard the TV ads: "You don't want your mother's hump, do you?"

Because vertebral compressions so often cause little in the way of symptoms and because they are not dangerous, I beg your pardon for ignoring them in the following analysis. I do not mean to slight those of you who have painful or deforming disease of the spine.

By contrast, hip fractures do cause significant morbidity, disability, and sometimes even mortality. According to the May 2011 review on clinicalevidence.com, about 13 percent of people die in the year after a hip fracture, and most survivors lose some or all of their previous independence. For this reason I'll focus only on the benefits, risks and costs of three drugs and their effect on non-vertebral fracture prevention.

Just one or two more things, then I promise to get to the table. Clinicalevidence.com, one of the least biased and most highly respected and trusted sources of information about the effects of different treatments, rates the quality of the *evidence* on the biphosphonates as "very low" or "moderate." That just means they find substantial defects in the methods used to conduct the clinical experiments or to report the results. In plain English, one must use caution in applying the results to people in the general population.

Another reason to consider these results as "preliminary" rests in the fact that the clinical trials were sponsored by the firms manufacturing the drugs. Dr. David Newman of Mt. Sinai School of Medicine reminds us that the pharmaceutical industry has "a

Brittle Bones: a Bonanza for Big Pharma

long history of selective outcome reporting, and of occasionally fraudulent reporting." His website thennt.com provides a good review of the biphosphonates from a May 16, 2011 review of the literature.

The second word of caution applies to the likelihood—the chance or the odds if you will—that a white woman (the other races are rarely affected by osteoporosis) will suffer a fracture of the hip or wrist. About 15 percent will break a wrist, and 18 percent a hip over a lifetime.

The clinical trials, of course, last only about five or ten years, not a lifetime. They always compare at least two groups of patients—those who take a biphosphonate and those who take a placebo (sugar pill). To put things into a perspective we can get our minds around, only ten out of a hundred of the patients who take the placebo sustain fractures, on average, over three years time. Finally, the researchers reveal one more interesting thing. The drugs offer no protection against fractures to white women who have normal bone density or to those who have not suffered a previous fracture.

Drug Used	Reduction in Fractures	NNT Prevent One Fracture	Harms from Treatment
Actonel tablet daily, weekly or monthly	1% (10% placebo vs. 9% Actonel had fractures)	100 for 3 years	stomach ulcers (3%); heartburn, gas (27%)
Fosamax tablet daily or weekly	2% (11% placebo vs. 9% Fosamax had fractures)	50 for 3 years	stomach ulcers (3%); heartburn, gas (28%)
Reclast injection once annually	3% (11% placebo vs. 8% Reclast had fractures)	33 for 3 years	atrial fibrillation (1.3%); fever and flu-like symptoms (10–15%) kidney failure (1.2%)

And One Pill Makes You Small

Now in English

Using Fosamax as an example to guide you in the interpretation of this too complex chart, here is what it means to you. Your doctor says, "Your bone scan shows you have osteoporosis, and one of your vertebrae is compressed." Imagine yourself in a room with ninety-nine other women who get the same news. What, you wonder, are the chances I, personally, will get a serious fracture because my bones are thin?

Well, over the next three years, eleven of you will break a hip or a wrist if you don't take Fosamax every week (column two). That's the *likelihood or probability* of your getting a fracture if you don't take the drug. It also means eighty-nine of you will not break your hip or wrist in the next three years— even if you don't take the pill.

Not one to take any risks, you're thinking you'd better take the doctor up on her offer to prescribe Fosamax for you. Now imagine you're in a different room with forty-nine other women (column three) who have also decided to take the prescription for three years. For *one* of you the Fosamax will prevent a broken hip or wrist. The other forty-nine will get no benefit from it, even if you take it faithfully for three years. (You might be thinking the Medicare prescription drug benefit is a lot like the lottery.)

Fosamax is relatively safe, but for each one hundred people who take it, three will get stomach ulcers. Twenty-eight of one hundred will have symptoms like heartburn, gas or belching (column four).

In 2006 a research team at UC San Francisco extends the study period for Fosamax an additional five years. During that time the same number of postmenopausal women sustain hip or wrist fractures whether they keep taking Fosamax or not. It appears from this experiment that Fosamax protects a very small number of women who take it for up to five years. After that the doctors observe no protection from fractures whatsoever.

Brittle Bones: a Bonanza for Big Pharma

Calcium and Vitamin D

What about the vitamin D that Mrs. Olsen is taking? Does it prevent broken bones in post-menopausal women? Clinicalevidence. com states, "Vitamin D taken by itself is unlikely to be beneficial." Dr. Newman's review of May 15, 2011 concurs. The only possible exceptions, he adds, are frail, elderly people in nursing homes.

Some high quality trials show a small benefit from taking calcium (500–1200 milligrams a day) plus vitamin D3 (more than 700 international units a day) in this group of people. Taking either alone provides no protection against fractures in the best clinical trials, but taking them together prevents one hip fracture in every forty-two patients.

So how did Vitamin D get so hot? This nutrient occurs naturally in some of the foods found in a well-balanced diet, especially fish, milk, and eggs. The sun also contributes to the daily production of vitamin D in our skin.

Could government again be an accomplice or even a culprit in promoting the popularity of this natural nutrient? According to the National Institutes of Health, "As little as ten minutes of exposure is thought to prevent deficiencies . . . because vitamin D3 is synthesized by humans in the skin when it's exposed to sunlight . . . The major biologic function of vitamin D is maintaining normal blood levels of calcium and phosphorus; vitamin D may provide protection from osteoporosis, high blood pressure, cancer and several autoimmune diseases."

Wow! That's a sweeping endorsement of the sunshine vitamin. Residents of Seattle are probably feeling shortchanged.

As we will see in Chapter 5, government initiatives often lead to widespread changes in diets and behaviors that cannot be backed up by the best science. It seems we humans have a herd mentality in these matters.

We expect Big Pharma to toot its horn for its products, and in a free market economy we embrace the legitimacy of advertising. Our freedoms include the right for willing buyers and sellers to come together in commercial transactions, but *caveat emptor* applies here as it does in all our decisions to buy things.

Listen to this statement I found when I searched Medscape. com using the word "osteoporosis" on January 13, 2015. (Medscape is WebMD's site for professionals—pharmacists, doctors, and nurses—to find information on diseases and current treatments.) Then I'll break it down.

"Osteoporosis represents an increasingly serious health and economic problem in the United States and around the world." A few years ago this same website dramatized that osteoporosis was a "public health problem."

A public health problem exists when someone has a disease they can unknowingly transmit to another person. A classic example is tuberculosis. The patient with an active Mycobacterium tuberculosis infection presents a danger to other members of his community, because the disease is communicable; it is contagious. He can infect others through his respiratory secretions just by close contact with them. That is a public health problem.

A woman with thinning of her bones cannot transmit thin bones to any other human being, so she doesn't present a threat to the health of the public. By giving this status to a risk factor like osteoporosis, the drug makers—from whom Medscape gets most of its revenue through paid advertising—scare us with their shameless disease mongering.

It is true that, in the broken world we live in, about fifteen out of every one hundred white women will suffer a hip or wrist fracture in their lifetime; but biphosphonate drugs like Fosamax, Actonel, and Reclast help only a small fraction of them avoid the suffering such an injury causes. Playing the role of healthy skeptic as you navigate the medical system will lead to better decision making for you and those who love and care for you.

CHAPTER 5

Clean Arteries, Clean Heart

Blessed are the pure in heart, for they shall see God.

MATTHEW 5:8

I have known Isabella since she was in her twenties. Not long ago she called to tell me she had moved back to Virginia to live nearer her children, and was having trouble getting her Medicare health plan transferred. We talked a while about her medical problems, and she expressed some frustration with her current physician, an internal medicine practitioner.

He was pressuring her, she said, to increase the dosage of her Lipitor to reduce her cholesterol even further. She didn't want to because she had noticed some intense pain in the muscles of her legs the last few months, and she had heard that might be a side effect of Lipitor. She reluctantly admitted she thought she had some "brain malfunction" as well. Her memory and her ability to think things through had fallen off sharply in the last year or two.

She asked my opinion about the "statin" drugs, of which Lipitor is the best seller. (It is also the world's all time biggest selling drug.) I suggested she gather up her medical records, which she had wisely requested before she moved, and call me back with some specific test results. A couple of days later she telephoned me with her cholesterol numbers, which I have reproduced with her permission.

Date	Total Cholesterol	Ratio Total:HDL Cholesterol
1999	220	3.6
2000	276	3.9
2001	227	4
2007	184	2.9
2008 March	240	4.1
2008 April	223	4.1
2008 June	217	4.3

Because I've been looking at test results for about forty years now, a few things from this table jump out at me immediately. Before I get to that, however, it seems good to focus on the big picture first. Isabella is subconsciously asking a simple question: What are the odds I will have a heart attack or stroke if I take my doctor's advice to increase the dosage, and what are the odds if I do not? What if I just stop taking Lipitor altogether?

She is also wondering if the symptoms she described above are related to taking Lipitor, and if they will disappear if she stops taking it. Oh, yes, she worries too about the cost of the drug, since she is retired and living on a fixed income now. I hope some of you are asking the same questions. It's a sign of a healthy skepticism to do so. Being the systematic personality I am, here is how my mind was working Isabella's question out. You can work it out for yourself in the same manner.

First I had to calculate the odds—or in the jargon of medicine, the risk—that she would have a stroke or heart attack in the future. Of course, no one but our Creator knows that, but we can apply science to the question and make some estimates. The best known risk calculator, the Framingham Study, has been around since 1948. I went to their website while I was on the phone with Isabella and typed in her numbers.

I informed her that her chance of having a cardiovascular event in the next ten years was 3 percent. I'll say it another way. If you take a hundred women of her age group who are not smokers and who have normal blood pressure, and who have similar cholesterol ratios as those shown in the table above, in the next ten years three of them will have a heart attack if they take no drugs to reduce the cholesterol levels in their blood.

She paused and said, "That's not very likely is it?"

I replied, "Only slightly more likely than winning the lottery."

Marketing Math

Surprised? I was too until I began analyzing clinical studies for a living a few years ago. You might be wondering how what I've been telling you squares with the ads you see on television and in the newspaper. One features the inventor of the artificial heart, Dr. Robert Jarvik. He is promoting Pfizer's lipid-lowering blockbuster, Lipitor, which he presumably takes himself. The ad says Lipitor reduces the risk of heart attack by 36 percent.

How did Pfizer arrive at that conclusion, when the best clinical study (the West of Scotland Study) done in people without heart disease reports that statins prevent only one heart attack for every two hundred people treated? The small type in Pfizer's print ads says that 3 percent of people (three out of one hundred) in the clinical trial have heart attacks in the group taking the placebo, the sugar pill. In the group taking Lipitor, 2 percent have heart attacks. Most of us would say that the real pill reduces the incidence of heart attacks by 1 percent, or that for every one hundred people who take the pill one heart attack is avoided. In the business, we call that the absolute risk reduction. (This term is very important; remember it.)

The drug manufacturers know that won't impress anybody, so they use a figure called the *relative risk* reduction to make their products sound more powerful. Here's how they derive it: three heart attacks occur in the control group, two in the study group. That difference is one heart attack per hundred. Divide one by three (the number of heart attacks in the group that takes the dummy pill) and you get a 33.3 percent reduction. Pretty slick. Imagine that your bank tells you they are going to pay you 50 percent higher interest on your savings account; your ears perk up. But when you get down there to sign up, you find they are raising the rate from 2 percent to 3. You look confused, and your banker reassures you that a 1 percent increase from the original two percent (one divided by two) equals 0.5, or a 50 percent raise!

Returning to the West of Scotland trial, it finds an absolute risk reduction of one-half of 1 percent, or 0.005. I will remind you, because this is not intuitive, that this means that for every two hundred people who take the lipid lowering drug, one heart attack is prevented.

Now you can see why Big Pharma (the drug manufacturers, collectively) uses the *relative* risk reduction in the sales process. Imagine telling a room filled with two hundred people that you want them to take your pill every day for the rest of their lives. They will have to pay thousands of dollars a year in drug costs and doctors' visits with lab tests. About 10 percent (20) of them will suffer side effects like disabling muscle pain or confusion. Four of them (2 percent) will develop diabetes, a serious chronic disease, within the next five years. A few of them will sustain damage to their liver because they take the drug, and one hundred ninety-nine of them will get *no benefit* from it at all.

Most of you will not fall for it. How did it happen, then, that in 2011 more than twenty million Americans filled prescriptions for the cholesterol lowering drugs called "statins"?

Big Brother Is Watching Us

Business Week magazine published an informative expose on the lipid religion in its January 28, 2008, issue. Reporter John Carey titled his article "Do Cholesterol Drugs Do Any Good?" Here are a few notable quotes and facts from the piece:

- Dr. James M. Wright, a professor at the University of British Columbia, finds that people *without* heart disease are the largest users of the drugs, yet those over age sixty-five got no benefit from them no matter how much their cholesterol dropped. His team of analysts finds no benefit for women of any age. As in the Scotland trial, he finds a tiny drop in the heart attack rate among middle-aged men taking statins, but the *death rate* in the group taking the pill is the same as in the group taking the placebo, or dummy pill. Dr. Wright concludes: "Most people are taking something with no chance of benefit and a risk of harm."

- The Pfizer study showing a 36 percent reduction in heart attacks uses carefully selected patients with several risk factors along with high cholesterol. Many smoke cigarettes and have high blood pressure. By contrast, the only large trial funded by the government finds no benefit to the drugs at all.

- Dr. Nortin M. Hadler, professor of medicine at the University of North Carolina, explains that studies showing only small benefits are always uncertain. Several recent papers published in reputable medical journals reveal that patients at lower risk of heart disease—not diabetic, not smokers, with normal blood pressure—get even less benefit than previously thought. Maybe as many as two hundred and fifty people have to take a statin for five years or more to prevent one heart attack. We consider that a very large NNT, or number-needed-to-treat.

- Some therapies, by contrast, have a very small NNT. For example, we know a bacterium in the stomach causes ulcers. To heal one ulcer with an antibiotic cocktail, you need to treat only five patients. This cocktail is *efficacious*. Statins are not.

- In several small studies, people who switch to a Mediterranean diet and exercise more have fewer heart attacks than people who take statins. (The small number of participants in these trials requires caution in generalizing the results to large groups of people, however).

- Dr. Rodney A. Hayward, professor of internal medicine at University of Michigan, says, "It is almost impossible to find someone who believes strongly in statins who does not get a lot of money from industry" (another name for the drug makers).

- Dr. Ronald M. Krauss at Oakland Research Institute reminds us that cholesterol is just one of many risk factors for developing heart disease. "When you look at patients with heart disease, their cholesterol levels are not that much higher than those without heart disease," he says. Spaniards have cholesterol levels similar to Americans, but less than half the rate of heart disease.

- Even more distressing to some of us is this last fact: the rush to reduce the cholesterol level in the bloodstreams of Americans comes from a federal government initiative, the National Cholesterol Education Program (NCEP). They think statins are so powerful that forty million of us ought to be taking them. Their survey in 1999—2000 reveals that one of every four Americans is either on a statin or has high cholesterol.

The Medical Arms Race

I have a friend who is a hospital administrator. He compares the current medical environment to the Cold War era that followed the Korean conflict. Those of you old enough to remember the tension of the Bay of Pigs Invasion, Sputnik satellites orbiting the earth, and Checkpoint Charlie will recognize some of the same fears when you watch drug ads on television today. With its exorbitant growth and price inflation, the Medical/Industrial Complex has caught up with President Dwight D. Eisenhower's Military/Industrial Complex.

When the Congress created Medicare and Medicaid through a legislative act in 1965, the world of medicine changed profoundly. This change made explicit what had been unspoken for generations: the practice of medicine is first and foremost a commercial enterprise. We doctors, the drug and device makers, and the hospital industry, provide a service for which people are willing to pay a price, and we are in business to make money.

When I graduated from medical school in 1969, we measured patients' cholesterol levels, and we considered anything below three hundred to be normal. In 1985, twenty years after the enactment of Medicare, the government changed the definition of normal. The National Institutes of Health (NIH) launched the National Cholesterol Education Program (NCEP—you will get used to these acronyms if you stick around long enough). Its mission: to reduce illness and death from coronary heart disease (CHD) in the United States by reducing the percent of Americans with high blood cholesterol. They decreed that "Normal Shall Now Be Two Hundred and Forty," and added that "You're better off if you get it down to two hundred."

They figured about 25 percent of us have high cholesterol and more than half have levels above the most desirable cutoff of two hundred. Dr. James Cleeman, the NCEP director, said, "It's a mammoth intervention, and it deserves to be a mammoth intervention." They enlisted the aid of the American Heart Association, the American College of Cardiology, and the American Medical Association to get the message out.

At the time it escaped our attention that those groups have strong financial incentives to make the campaign the rousing success it has become. Health journalist Robert J. Davis, PhD, teaches at Emory University's School of Public Health, and he wrote a very helpful book in 2008 entitled "The Healthy Skeptic." Professor Davis attributes much of the triumph to the conversion of high cholesterol from a risk factor to a serious condition.

Viewed in this light, we are more likely to think of it as a disease, much like asthma or arthritis. It is not a disease, but one among several risk factors for the development of coronary artery disease. He said in this book, "Turning high cholesterol into an illness is an example of . . . disease mongering, stretching the definition of disease so that more people get labeled as sick and require medical treatment."

Gradually the NCEP has revised its treatment protocols to include an ever growing number of Americans. According to Prof. Davis, the 2001 edition of the guidelines nearly triples the potential population of drug recipients, going from thirteen to thirty-six million. Three years later it expands the universe of "patients" even further by calling for more aggressive use of statins, which are already the top selling class of drugs in the nation.

Objection!

Not all the experts agree with the direction the NIH has taken. Two dissenting doctors carried out their own analysis of the best clinical trials and came up with an entirely different interpretation. Dr. John Abramson, of Harvard, and Dr. James Wright from the University of British Columbia pooled the results from eight randomized, controlled trials (the "gold standard" in medical research) of statin use in primary prevention. (Primary prevention is another way of saying the subjects in the experiments did not have heart disease. Prescribing statins for patients with heart disease is termed secondary prevention.)

They revealed their findings in the British journal Lancet in 2007. Some of these conclusions might startle you. Some of you will go postal.

They find a very small benefit from statins in lowering the number of heart attacks in the group that takes them for five years. Compared to the group that takes the sugar pill, the absolute risk reduction (remember that)? is 1.5 percent over five years. One person out of sixty-seven avoids a heart attack or stroke—the other sixty-six get no benefit from the drug at all.

Even worse than the tiny reduction in heart attacks in the treated group is the stark fact that the death rate is the same in the group that gets the pill and the group that gets a placebo. That is to say the same number of people die no matter whether they take a statin or not. My interpretation of the data? Statins are a sixty-six to one long shot to prevent a heart attack, and they do not save any lives when taken by *people who do not have heart disease.*

Clean Arteries, Clean Heart

My female readers will not appreciate the revelation that women without heart disease get no help from statins in this analysis. The NCEP recommends that women without heart disease take statins, a position not supported by the best scientific evidence. It reminds Dr. Abramson of the push to get women on hormones after menopause. Doctors promote estrogen replacement without solid experimental evidence and make a travesty of the claims of American medicine to be based on the best science available (Davis, "The Healthy Skeptic," p. 102).

Wright and Abramson also find that healthy people age seventy and older do not appear to benefit from statins. Under NCEP guidelines the number of older people taking statins has jumped in recent years. More than 20 percent of folks sixty and over are on medication to reduce cholesterol, a higher proportion than among the 40–59 age group.

A couple of years ago, an old friend telephoned me in a very foul mood. Her mother's doctor had sent her to the drug store to fill a prescription for Lipitor. "My mother is ninety years old, for heaven's sake!" she screamed on the phone.

"Why does he want her to take it?" I asked, calm but concerned.

"He said they now think it might help prevent softening of the bones," she replied.

"What does your mother think about it?"

"She's irritated because she has to give up her daily grapefruit. It causes some kind of problem in getting the drug into her bloodstream," came the annoyed answer to my clinical question.

I then asked if her mother had raised the concern with her doctor.

"Of course not; she always just does what they tell her to do." The frustration in my friend's voice nearly fried the phone line.

I told her about the research I had done, that it lead me to believe Lipitor would not help her mother at all. I added, "The risk of it hurting her seems much greater than any chance of it helping to prevent heart problems."

And One Pill Makes You Small

Communication Breakdown

Led Zeppelin is one of my favorite classic vinyl bands. They think the root cause of trouble in relationships has something to do with a breakdown in communication. After the frustration reaches the breaking point, they scream "You drive me insane!" If going to the doctor today does not make you insane, you simply aren't paying attention.

I agreed to telephone her mother's doctor and talk it over with him. Our conversation can serve as a model for you to use if you are taking a lipid-lowering drug now and wondering if you should continue it indefinitely. Imagine yourself in your doctor's exam room, shivering in one of those thin, paper gowns, waiting for her to return and dispense her sage advice to you.

"Doctor," you start off, "I've been reading about the cholesterol drug you're prescribing for me." You're probably shaking like a leaf at this point, but you continue courageously. "You say I don't have any heart disease. There are quite a few articles coming out now saying that women my age cannot prevent heart trouble by taking these drugs."

"Well, you can't believe everything you read, you know," she replies without looking up, writing on your chart studiously.

"The things I read sound reliable to me," you continue, unabashed.

"Well, let's just stick with it for a while. When you come back for your blood test in three months, we'll talk about it again. OK?"

"You know, Doctor, I'm thinking I don't want to do that." Your newfound assertiveness astonishes you, but you feel energized, in control for a change, and you go on. "The evidence seems strong. If I'm getting any benefit at all from this drug, it is very small. My chances of having a heart attack, according to the risk calculator on the Framingham Heart Study (https://www.framingham-heartstudy.org), are really remote to begin with, and it is not clear the drugs lower the risk in women my age. I am paying more every year for the drug, and I'm about

52

to go broke—like the woman who sneaked up on Jesus in Mark 5:25. I'm going to stop taking it for now. When I come back in a year for my check up, maybe we can discuss it some more. OK?"

Your physician does not have time to argue with you. She blurts out, "It probably won't make any difference if you take it or not. I'll see you in a year, then."

You have taken back control of the temple!

Rewriting the Rules

I cannot tell you how often I hear stories just like this one. Widespread panic has gripped the nation! In 1998 the Journal of Family Practice published the results of a survey done on healthy, older Americans, to assess their attitudes about cholesterol and heart disease. The authors (Reddy, Kreher, and Hickner) find that 59 percent of people age sixty-five and older feel at least "slightly worried" about their cholesterol. (Half of them have normal or only slightly increased cholesterol readings.) One-third are at least moderately worried. Two-thirds are actively trying to keep their levels down with diet and exercise.

The cholesterol education program spawned by the National Institutes of Health is using professional marketing techniques to needlessly scare us. The NCEP website proclaims that people over 65 can "benefit greatly from lowering elevated cholesterol" and urges them to "keep their cholesterol low."

Drs. Abramson and Wright have joined thirty other physicians and research scientists in calling for the NIH to review the data on primary prevention again. It worries them that eight of the nine experts who wrote the 2004 rules for treatment received consulting fees and other financial incentives from the makers of statins. The table below lists the names of the experts and some of their industry connections. Wisdom demands avoiding even the appearance of wrong doing.

Dr. Brewer	Pfizer, Merck, Novartis	AstraZeneca, many more
Dr. Clark	Abbott, Bristol-Myers	Merck, Pfizer, others
Dr. Cleeman	No conflicts of interest	Director of the NCEP
Dr. Grundy	Merck, Bayer, Pfizer	Glaxo Smith Kline
Dr. Hunninghake	Merck, Novartis, Pfizer	Many more
Dr. Merz (AmCollegeCardiology)	Merck, Bayer, Pfizer	J&J, Medtronic, many more
Dr. Pasternak	Pfizer, Merck, Novartis	J&J, many more
Dr. Smith (Am Heart Asso)	Merck, Medtronic	Johnson and Johnson
Dr. Stone	Pfizer, Merck, Novartis	Schering-Plough, others

The buzz around cholesterol reminds me of Galileo. You remember him. In the year 1632 his science shocks the sensibilities of the nobility and the church in Italy upon his publication of a "Dialogue Concerning the Two Chief World Systems." He audaciously proclaims that the earth revolves around the sun, not vice versa. The church imprisoned him for his heliocentric heresy.

(Now, reports The Wall Street Journal, an anonymous donor wants to commission a statue of Galileo to reside in the Vatican. The paper quotes Monsignor Melchor Sanchez de Toca, of the Vatican's Pontifical Council for Culture, as remarking, "Galileo is like a Mexican soap opera; it never ends.")

That's just the way I feel about cholesterol theories. Today the scientific community indicts cholesterol as *the* primary culprit in coronary artery disease. It glosses over the fact that many heart attack patients have normal cholesterol levels. There is more to this than meets the eye. Cholesterol occurs *naturally* in our bodies. Our Creator designed it as a building material for the membranes which surround the contents of our body's cells. Cholesterol has a role in making hormones. Our brains contain a lot of cholesterol.

Changing the amounts of this naturally occurring cholesterol causes calamity on occasion. Our muscle cells undergo destruction.

The Food and Drug Administration (FDA) made the manufacturer of one of the statins, Baycol, take it off the market when they discovered it was causing muscle damage in too many patients. Then, in February 2012, the FDA made official what patients have long known—statin use causes memory loss and confusion. Then, they admitted, it also causes diabetes in some patients! These risks violate the time honored maxim in medicine: "First, do no harm."

Emory's Professor Davis points the way for us to find resources he believes to be trustworthy. Investigating one of them, the Center for Medical Consumers, I find it is giving reliable information. It works with the Cochrane Group, a team of researchers who analyze and report on the evidence for the most common treatments. I rely on the Cochrane Collaboration, and I almost always find it to be accurate and informative. The website for Medical Consumers is http://www.medicalconsumers.org. I recommend it to you.

A few pages back I talked about a statistic called NNT, the number of people you need to treat to prevent one problem. David Newman, MD, from his base at Mt. Sinai School of Medicine in New York, operates a website called "the NNT." (You can view it on the web at www.thennt.com.) The November 2, 2013 update of the evidence quantifies the benefits and risks of treating people without known heart disease for five years with a statin drug. He concludes after reviewing the best studies to date: No Lives Are Saved!

- 1 in 60 are HELPED by preventing a non-fatal heart attack
- 1 in 268 are HELPED by preventing a stroke
- 1 in 50 are HARMED by developing diabetes
- 1 in 10 are HARMED by muscle damage

Just Give Me the Good News

Some of my critics ask me if I think there are any good remedies to offer people. Yes, I do. In the table below I list the actual risk and the NNT for some other cardiovascular diseases to give you an idea of the variation in available therapies. (You, yourself, can calculate the NNT if you know the absolute risk reduction—ARR—the number of unpleasantries avoided for every one hundred people treated. Divide that number into the number one. If the absolute risk reduction is three per hundred the NNT is 1 divided by 0.03 = 33).

Disease	Treatment	NNT
Death from Congestive Heart Failure	ACE Inhibitors (drugs like lisinopril) for 3 years	25, so ARR= 0.04 or 4%; 23% of patients on ACEI died, 27% on placebo
Stroke Prevention in people with symptoms of carotid artery blockage (either a recent stroke or a TIA)	Surgical clean out when carotid artery is at least 70% blocked (but not almost totally blocked)	6, so ARR= .16 or 16%; 10% had strokes after surgery; 26% of those not having surgery had strokes NNT rises to 21 if artery is only 50–69% blocked

Be Alert!

The action in the cardiac medical arms race is now shifting to a new front—diabetes. The physician education division of Web MD sent this news flash to me a few years ago (July 2008). (Warning: the majority of Web MD's revenue comes from advertisements paid for by the drug and device makers.) The American Association of Clinical Endocrinologists (AACE) commands us to view pre-diabetics in the same way as diabetics regarding intensive lifestyle management and setting targets for lowering blood pressure and lipid levels. Not surprisingly, the feds are leading the charge again. The first goal is aggressive lifestyle management to prevent the progression to type 2 diabetes, following guidelines from the Diabetes Prevention Program of the US government.

The doctors are scrambling to implement the new rules. "As individuals and as a society, we need to address those forces which are creating the epidemic of obesity, diabetes, and pre-diabetes,"

Yehuda Handlesman, MD FACP, FACE, treasurer of AACE and medical director of the Metabolic Institute of America, says in a news release. "We understand the difficulties in implementing solutions, but as an association of endocrinologists we are committed to supporting community and national efforts in every way we can." Dr. Handlesman resists the urge to gloat: "It doesn't hurt to increase our annual patient visits either."

Regarding intensive lifestyle management, another member of the organization puts a different twist on the debate. "Although lifestyle can clearly modify the progression of patients towards overt diabetes, it may not be sufficient," says Alan J. Garber, MD, PhD, FACE, professor of medicine, Baylor College of Medicine in Houston, Texas, and chairman of the Consensus Conference. "Medications may well be required, particularly in high risk groups."

People, get ready; there's a train a' comin'. Amylin Pharmaceuticals, Inc., Daiichi Sankyo, Inc., GlaxoSmithKline, LifeScan, Inc., Merck & Co, Inc., Novo Nordisk Inc., and Roche Laboratories Inc. support this consensus statement. The article goes on to say, "Although the US prevalence of pre-diabetes . . . exceeds 56 million, an even larger number of individuals with pre-diabetes is still undiagnosed."

The founders of the American republic said something to this effect: "Constant vigilance is the price we must pay for freedom." Washington, Jefferson, Madison, and Franklin had never heard of diabetes, but their wisdom applies to medicine as well as to politics and citizenship, two hundred and thirty years later. One expert extolls the virtues of diet and exercise; another doubts they will be sufficient. Tune your television to any of the news networks. The host is interviewing a medical doctor, call him Dr. Rosenberg, who's explaining a recently published diet study. The goal is weight loss and reduction of body mass index. The study group and the comparison group both exercise regularly and diet. The study group takes the added step of eating two eggs for breakfast every morning. The egg eaters lose more weight, and have more "energy," than those who do not eat eggs. Amazing!

And One Pill Makes You Small

I am willing to bet that Dr. Rosenberg has told his patients ten thousand times over the last twenty years, "Do not eat eggs; they have too much cholesterol." That's been medical dogma since the NCEP promulgated its first guidelines in the mid–eighties. Today he is praising the health benefits of eggs!

The purveyors of medical care are breaking promises they made to the American people. Some Christians saw this coming. The Bible warns us about it in the instructions Paul writes to his protege Timothy, who is setting up missionary churches. I especially like Eugene Peterson's translation of this passage from The Message (1 Timothy 4):

> "The Spirit makes it clear that as time goes on, some are going to give up on the faith and chase after demonic illusions put forth by professional liars. These liars have lied so well and for so long that they've lost their capacity for truth. They will tell you not to get married. They'll tell you not to eat this or that food— perfectly good food God created to be eaten heartily and with thanksgiving by Christians! Everything God created is good, and to be received with thanks. Nothing is to be sneered at and thrown out . . . Exercise daily in God—no spiritual flabbiness, please! Workouts in the gym are useful, but a disciplined life in God is far more so, making you fit both today and forever. You can count on this. Take it to heart."

Not to belabor the point made in Chapter 3, but God has prepared a better plan for his people. The God-man, Jesus Christ, is faithful in keeping all his promises. In the Sermon on the Mount, sometimes called the Beatitudes, Jesus says, "Blessed are the pure in heart, for they shall see God" (Matthew 5:8). He is describing an attitude, not an artery or an anatomic structure. Exactly what is this attitude Jesus talks about? At its root, it is a desire to please God. So how can we know if we have this spiritual pulse? We know he has given us a new, pure heart if we love his commandments, his precepts and his laws.

Luke, the physician–turned–gospel writer, records that Jesus says in another sermon words to the effect that you cannot add a single hour to your span of life by being anxious. When his preaching and healing ministry on earth is completed, he sheds his blood so ours will be clean.

If we are healed by his wounds, as the apostle Peter writes, can we not trust him to provide everything we need in this world and the next? If you believe he died for your sins and his Father raised him from the dead, you are clean in the sight of God. He has given you a new heart, just as he promised through the prophets. God has not given us a spirit of fear, but of power and of love, and of a sound mind. We can use common sense and science along with Scripture. Neither paralyzed by a painful past nor fearful of an indefinite future, we can move forward boldly with the sure confidence he will do everything he has promised us.

CHAPTER 6

Follow The Money

And there was a woman who had had a discharge of blood for twelve years, and who had suffered much under many physicians, and had spent all that she had, and was no better but rather grew worse.

MARK 5:25–26

We saw earlier that the use of certain treatments varies a lot among the 306 hospital referral regions in the United States. It follows logically that spending on medical care will also vary widely. Americans spend more per person than any other nation in the world—$8,508 at latest count in 2011 (OECD data). In second place is Norway at $5,669 per person. The tenth place country is France, who spends $4,118 per capita.

Looking through the lens of expenses as a percentage of GDP (what a nation makes) the USA is, again, the blue ribbon winner. In 2011 we spent over two and a half trillion dollars, or 17.7 percent of GDP. Norway spent 9.3 percent, and Luxembourg 8.2 percent. Someone will say that Americans are healthier, so the enormous expenses are worth it.

Follow The Money

Diving deep into the data, I find that assertion to be spurious. Our life expectancy at birth is lower than twenty-five of the thirty-four developed nations of the world, and we lead all countries in obesity by a wide margin.

The researchers at Dartmouth University in New Hampshire have compiled a remarkable number of studies in their Dartmouth Atlas Of Health Care (www.dartmouthatlas.org). They are using Medicare data to compare the patterns of medical care and the expense of treating older Americans from sea to shining sea. (Lest you think Americans who are not elderly have a different experience, the commercial insurance data show a virtually indistinguishable pattern.) Depending on where seniors get their care for the most complex problems—brain and heart surgery—the nation is divided into three hundred and six hospital referral regions.

These data show a large variation in spending on behalf of the seniors in those three hundred and six regions. One of the most fascinating findings in their studies shows that regions *with more doctors and hospitals* spend more money on medical care. This difference in *capacity* accounts for the differences in spending much more than how old or sick or poor the people are. The Dartmouth website euphemistically states, "Regional variation in hospital and physician capacity reveals the irrational distribution of valuable and expensive health care resources. Capacity strongly influences both the quantity and per capita cost of care provided to patients."

Some critics of the Dartmouth Atlas contend the *poor* are sicker, and therefore have higher medical expenses. It is true, on average, that the poor have higher spending, but this only accounts for 4 percent of the difference between high and low cost areas of the country. People with low incomes also have less access to effective treatments, offsetting some of the higher spending required by their diseases.

Other critics say that the higher spending areas have more sick people, regardless of income. They fail to recognize, however, that many diagnoses are made *because of* more intense testing and doctor visits in high use and cost areas. A lot of those diagnoses have little or no impact on the patient's health status. This bias only makes it appear that people in high cost areas are sicker. If you study groups of patients with *similar illnesses*, you still find more than a two-fold variation in the number of services rendered to them in different areas of the U. S.

The evidence compiled in the Dartmouth Atlas is conclusive: most of the difference in spending is due to differences in the *use of the hospital as a site of care*. (Patients use alternate sites of care such as hospices, nursing homes, or primary care doctors' offices less in the high cost areas.) The use of hospital care also generates more visits by specialist physicians and more tests. This spending *does not* lead to better outcomes for patients, and it can cause real trouble. More on that later.

A color-coded map of the USA shows that the highest Medicare expenses per enrollee are concentrated in a line from Pennsylvania to Texas. This line especially includes Kentucky, Mississippi, and Louisiana. New York, New Jersey, and Florida round out the East-Coast big spenders, and Los Angeles/Las Vegas stands out like a sore thumb on the map of the West. Several regions within each of these states incur expenses that put them in the top tier— between $10,525 and $13,596 per enrollee in 2012. (All spending is adjusted for the age, sex, and race of the population and for regional differences in prices.)

By contrast, the lowest cost regions spend from $6,724 to $8,264 per enrollee. Those regions are located in the northern tier of states stretching from Minnesota to Oregon and northern California.

When you multiply this difference in cost by the number of enrollees in a region, some startling sums begin to emerge. The highest cost region in the contiguous forty-eight states is Miami, Florida. The average cost for the 158,292 enrollees in 2012 was $13,596. The lowest cost region was Bend, Oregon whose 26,056 Medicare enrollees averaged $6,781. If the doctors in Miami will practice medicine at the same level of intensity as the doctors in Bend, the American taxpayers will save just over one billion dollars. In one year alone!

But, the American people suffer from a bias which can be stated as "more medical care is always better." This predilection leads to much unnecessary risk and cost in the consumption of medical services. For example, the decision whether to treat a patient in the hospital or as an outpatient hinges, for most common *medical* conditions, on the local supply of hospital beds. (The local supply of beds, on the other hand, has only a modest influence on the relative risk of being hospitalized for *surgical* conditions.) This factor can be stated as "build it and they will come."

In communities that have an excessive number of hospitals, the doctors almost always err on the side of "more care is better." People living in regions that have more beds get more admissions to the hospital; people in regions with more specialists get more visits to specialists; those in regions with more CT scanners receive more cat scans.

In regions where there are fewer medical resources, patients get less care; however, there is no evidence these patients are worse off than those in the higher use/spending areas. The Dartmouth authors conclude that "patients do not experience improved survival or better quality of life if they live in regions with more care. In fact, the care they receive appears to be worse. They report being less satisfied with their care than patients in regions that spend less, and having more trouble getting in to see their physicians."

What's worse, this supply-sensitive care also accounts for *more than half* of all Medicare spending. The low cost area mentioned earlier—Bend, Oregon—has about 30 percent *fewer* acute care beds than the national average. Another high cost region—Kingsport, Tennessee—has almost 60 percent *more* beds than the average. Unsurprisingly, they rank at the top of the chart on a measure Dartmouth titles "Hospital Discharges per 1,000 Medicare Enrollees."

Region	Hospital Discharges/1000
Kingsport, TN	329
Miami, FL	252
Bend, OR	112
National Average	209

Hospitals Can Be Dangerous Places

The high *cost* of receiving care in a hospital instead of an outpatient setting is not the only problem; hospitals are increasingly becoming more dangerous. Medical errors, adverse events, and antibiotic-resistant infections lead the list of perils facing those who receive their treatment as inpatients. Until recently, just the mention of methicillin-resistant Staphylococcus aureus scared the daylights out of us. Now we're battling an even scarier tribe of "super bugs"—the intestinal bacteria that are impervious to the carbapenem antibiotics. A 2010 article on WebMD reveals that 48,000 Americans *die* annually from infections they contract while in the hospital for something else. That's three times more than die from HIV infections, they go on to say.

A search on February 26, 2015 led me to an article on the website of the Centers for Disease Control (CDC). They say it's getting worse—now 99,000 people a year die—and approximately 1.7 million hospital acquired infections occur each year. That's not what I call a long shot.

Other risks creep in the moment you move into a hospital bed. As more physicians get involved in your care, it becomes less clear who is in charge. That leads to miscommunication, and mistakes become more likely. More intense diagnostic testing increases the odds of finding things that are unlikely to cause the patient any problems. When your doctor finds something—*anything*—unexpected, more invasive procedures usually ensue. Often a biopsy is ordered, and those resulting incisions sometimes get infected. When the incision gets red, they put you on antibiotic drugs which occasionally cause systemic allergic reactions. A few reactions are even fatal. A colonoscopy carries the risk of perforating the microbial-laden large intestine. The germs escape through the new hole in the bowel wall and quickly set up house keeping in your abdominal cavity; hours later a diffuse, very morbid—and sometimes mortal—infection is raging. These adverse effects are termed *iatrogenic errors*, from the Greek words translated "your physician caused this."

Ten Things Hospitals Won't Tell You

This headline appeared on the home page of my web browser on February 21, 2015. Market Watch, a free publication of the Wall Street Journal, likes to use these "ten things" lists to attract viewers; this one caught me.

A few of the things you might find surprising include the hospitals' inability to find out what a procedure is going to cost before you are put under anesthesia. They also won't know if your insurance plan covers it. Oh, and don't expect hospital doctors to communicate to your primary care physician what they did to you while you were there.

Number Six? That Place is infection city.

Enough said. You get the picture.

The article concludes with the advice to "have somebody with you at all times." This helps to keep theft of personal items down. Your personal attendant can also make staff aware of advance directives you've drawn up, including Do Not Resuscitate orders. Not that this will do any good. The staff often ignores such orders, and they joke that DNR stands for Did Not Read. (That happened in real life two years ago, when my wife went to the hospital with her mother. She had a broken hip, so her dutiful daughter went armed with the Power of Attorney and Advanced Medical Directives. Read all about it in the last chapter of this book—The Final Battle).

And One Pill Makes You Small

How Doctors Generate Business

The flip side of the inpatient hospital coin is the medical specialist. No one can be admitted to, or discharged from, a hospital without a doctor's order. How many doctors does it take to care for a patient in the hospital? (I'm not jesting.) It depends on where you live—geography is everything. Looking at the variation in the use of medical specialists across the three hundred and six regions in the U. S., Dartmouth's researchers describe very large differences in the number of visits. In some cases, these differences exist even among cities within a single state. Before I parse the data, keep in mind they are only for *medical specialists*; PCPs and surgeons are not included.

For the sake of consistent comparison, I am using Florida for this analysis because it contains the highest overall spending region in the nation—Miami. The report measures the number of visits to medical specialists—*in the last two years of life*—for deceased Medicare beneficiaries in each of the eighteen hospital referral regions in Florida. They use this group of patients because they all get the same result—they die. Critics cannot say one patient was sicker than another.

The Florida state average is forty visits per decedent (deceased Medicare beneficiary). Miami and Fort Lauderdale tie for first with fifty-four visits per decedent in a two year period. Tallahassee has the fewest visits—nineteen. To say it another way, people in Miami/Fort Lauderdale go nearly three times as often to specialists, on average, as those in Tallahassee.

Cities in the middle of the pack include Clearwater, Orlando, Jacksonville, and Tampa—all at forty visits, equalling the state average.

You might, at this juncture, be thinking the federal government could save us taxpayers some serious money by lowering the doctors' fees. When cutting the payment per visit is tried, the doctors keep their revenue steady by instructing the patients to come back more often. Can you see where this is going?

Follow The Money

Doctors control the flow of business in the medical complex, and they collect a fee for each face to face encounter with patients. Sometimes they put diagnostic machines in their offices to turbocharge the revenue generator.

One way to reduce the moral hazard inherent in fee-for-service medicine is to switch to a prospective payment system. Medicare did this with hospitals decades ago, and it immediately stopped the acceleration in the cost of inpatient care. When the financial incentive to keep patients coming back needlessly is no longer present, the variation in the number of visits to specialists will also shrink dramatically.

The number of visits will probably drop even in Tallahassee, because not all visits in that locale are essential to the health of the patient. For the sake of simplicity, though, let's assume for our experiment that the visit rate in Tallahassee remains at the 2008 to 2010 level of nineteen visits/decedent. As Miami and Fort Lauderdale scale back (since they will be paid a flat rate and will make no additional money on more visits), their rate will decline toward the state average of forty visits. How many *fewer* visits every two years do you imagine the specialists in those two cities will get if they operate at the average Florida level? An educated guess: close to 260,500 fewer visits. What will they do with all that spare time?

Root Causes of Runaway Costs

For decades now academics, government bureaucrats, managers of commercial health insurance plans, and wild-eyed prophets have delved into the mysteries behind the momentum of medical inflation. In the fullness of time it was revealed to them that the forces are legion. In this segment I'll try to summarize the most salient points from a mountain of research. This is not meant to be an academic treatise, but an effort to help remedy a practical thorn in everyone's flesh.

I usually think about these forces in terms of three broad categories.

- Perverse financial incentives for patients

- Government subsidies and regulation

- Monopoly privileges for doctors, hospitals, and drug makers

Perverse incentives cause patients to buy more insurance than they need—and doctors to order more services than are beneficial to those patients. Health insurance for the sake of a deduction from federal income taxes became popular after World War II. The government had put wage and price controls in place during the war. When our military men and women came home from the war, they needed jobs. Since the wages were fixed by the national government, businesses offered fringe benefits to attract the best workers. Those benefits included medical insurance. The money paid by the employer on behalf of a worker did *not count* as taxable income received by the employee. Seventy years later this feature of the tax code is still in place!

Imagine a system in which we pay our health insurance premiums out of *taxable income*. Since that money is no longer a deduction on our federal tax returns, we'll give serious consideration to how much we spend on insurance. We will buy only what we need and no more. We might lower our cost by increasing our deductible, for example. We do that when we buy insurance for our car or home; why not with medical insurance? The financial principle is the same.

With higher out-of-pocket costs, using *our own money* to pay for care, we will shop around for services when we need them. Suppose my orthopedic surgeon orders an MRI to diagnose my knee pain. Before I go to the hospital across the street from his office to get the imaging study, I will make a few phone calls. I live in Charlottesville, Virginia. It's only an hour's drive to Richmond, which has a lot more hospitals and more MRI machines to choose from. If a Richmond hospital, or a free-standing imaging center owned by some radiologists, quotes me a price several hundred dollars lower than my local hospital for the MRI, I'll drive to Richmond to get it done. On the way back home I'll stop at Short Pump Center, buy a new pair of shoes, and have lunch at Nordstrom's Cafe. That will leave me a couple of hundred dollars to the good and will cause providers to continue lowering their prices to get business like mine.

The second distortion of the medical economy comes as a result of regulations and subsidies. In the current environment, it is hard to buy insurance from a carrier in a neighboring state. Many of the services state legislatures and insurance commissions *mandate* must be covered are of no benefit to most people. *In vitro fertilization* comes to mind. The method of rating people's *risk* also differs from state to state. In some states you have to pay a lot more for your insurance if you have chronic medical conditions. Other states use community rating to set premiums, and it shields sicker people from having to pay higher premiums. Those states still allow insurers to charge certain occupational groups a higher premium to cover the higher risk inherent in their work. Roofers come to mind.

Most Americans get insurance through their employer, and several problems arise from this unique system. The tax treatment of money paid for premiums is not uniform among large employers, small ones, and individuals buying insurance on their own. Also, the insurance policy is terminated if you change jobs—you cannot take it with you.

Not only that, your employer might not offer the type of plan you are personally comfortable with. Healthy people who only go to doctors when they're sick might want to buy a very high deductible policy; they know it's unlikely they will use a lot of medical services.

The last of the three categories of causes of medical price inflation involves the protection of providers. All states, to my knowledge, have licensing requirements for doctors. You have to be a graduate of an "approved" medical college—that sort of thing. So far, so good. Those same state laws, however, make it illegal for you to obtain routine medical care—for coughs, colds, diarrhea, or diaper rash—from a lower-cost nurse or physician's assistant. In some states you cannot get treatment for back pain from a physical therapist unless a doctor orders it. That protects the chiropractor by granting a *monopoly* for her services.

And One Pill Makes You Small

Monopoly status extends beyond practitioners, even to the makers of drugs and devices. The Food and Drug Administration reserves the right to choose what treatments they will allow us to buy for ourselves and our families. That drives out lower-cost products that sometimes are just as safe and effective as those bearing the FDA seal of approval.

Copyright laws protect the creator of a new drug from competition for a number of years. Most new drugs are not more effective than older ones whose copyright protection has expired, but they are a *lot more expensive*. It amazes me that some drug makers can extend their protection of an expensive pill (cash cows they call them) by making a tiny modification of the molecule. For example, they change an isomer from a *d-* configuration to an *l*-design.

Hospitals enjoy a special form of monopoly privilege. Most states regulate the building of hospitals, the adding of beds, or the development of freestanding outpatient facilities through a Certificate of Need (CON) process. In this way established hospital systems can eliminate competition from start ups through the *political* process. They just have to persuade local committees of easily influenced citizens that "we really don't need any more hospital beds in our town." Or "we don't want the radiologists to build a freestanding imaging center; they can't do the quality control that we provide." The arguments against competition are limited only by the imagination.

A 12 Step Program to Cure High Costs

By now some of you have figured out we can dramatically lower the cost of care—by more than one-third—if we attack some of the root causes described above. Our addiction to expensive medical care can be broken by taking these simple steps.

- Break the link between health insurance and employment.

Follow The Money

- Free people to buy their own policies with after-tax dollars, so they can choose affordable plans that fit their personal preferences.

- Free people to use practitioners, without the requirement of state licensure.

- Free insurers to offer innovative insurance products across state lines.

- Break the monopolies enjoyed by drug makers, practitioners, and hospitals. Eliminate the approvals now required by FDA, CON, and state licensing boards.

- Break the link between the health insurance system and medical care to the indigent.

- Free local communities to provide care for their low income members as they see fit.

- Free people to negotiate directly with health care systems in their communities for the provision of medical services based on a prospective payment.

- Free people to choose treatments that conform to their personal preferences after full disclosure of the likely benefits and risks of all treatment options for their condition.

- Break the plaintiff lawyers' stranglehold on the medical malpractice system, and require the loser to pay court costs.

- Break the courts of awarding obscene monetary damages for pain and suffering.

- Use the Bible as a guide to limit such damages to a fair multiple of the actual economic loss.

CHAPTER 7

The Final Battle

_____

I am the Alpha and the Omega, the first and the last,
the beginning and the end.

REVELATION 22:13

A death in our family two years ago gave my wife and me a new perspective on medical care at the end of life. And it was *not* good. Ann's very ancient mother had been declining mentally for several years. As the dementia got progressively worse, she had several car wrecks. She also let strangers into her house, and they robbed her. We had asked her several times to move to Virginia and live with us. She always refused, saying she wanted to stay in Memphis where all her lifelong friends lived. At length she had to give up driving and living in her house. We found a nice independent living facility in her neighborhood and helped her move in. A hardcore shopper all her life, the stores she frequented were close by, and the van took the residents shopping a few days each week. Her motto: "If the van is going, I'm on it!"

After she had lived there eight years, we began getting reports that she was falling a lot. Then she fell and lay on the floor of her apartment for a day before she was discovered. She called me on the phone after she got up, and she was very confused. She kept saying, "I'm trying to call Dr. Crenshaw in Virginia."

I repeated three times, "This is Randy; you found me." She never understood.

We stopped what we were doing and took the thirteen-hour car ride to Memphis. Her mental clarity was definitely diminished when we arrived. The manager of the facility felt she could no longer live independently, so he gave us thirty days notice to find another place. The corporation that owned the independent facility had an opening in their assisted living facility (ALF) a few miles away, so we took it. The move was hard for her—and for us. At least we thought she would be safer here, because they gave her no access to cabs or cash.

Mother's mental status quickly declined, and she became incontinent. She had always been such a lady that she could not force herself to wear Depends. That complicated matters, because Ann couldn't take her out for the day for a change of scenery. Her bed was always wet. She didn't want people to think she was old, so she didn't use her walker. We stayed through Thanksgiving and Christmas, even though we weren't sure she knew who we were any longer.

The manager of the ALF mentioned hospice as a possible help for Mother. Neither Ann nor I had any knowledge of hospice—what it was, when people typically enrolled, etc.—so we were reluctant to investigate. We had always heard hospice was for terminal cancer patients. Plus, we had just had an increase in cost because we had moved from independent to assisted living, and we didn't really want to add to that by bringing in another caretaker. (We didn't know hospice would cost us nothing.) The manager didn't push us, perhaps because she didn't want to risk losing the revenue if hospice recommended moving Mother to a nursing home for her safety.

We returned to Virginia after Christmas. A week later the ALF called and said that Mother was not doing well. Expecting we'd have to put her in a nursing home, we headed the car back toward Tennessee. About the time we reached Knoxville, the car phone rang. The paramedics were certain she had suffered a hip fracture, so I instructed them to take her to the hospital in which she'd had her other hip fixed (three times). That's when the *medical machine* reared its ugly head.

The paramedics wanted to take her to the hospital next door. It was a different hospital system, and Mother's orthopedist didn't work there. Ann and I talked about it for a few minutes; persuaded that using the closest hospital would avoid a more painful transfer across town, we agreed. From there it got much worse.

Six hours later Ann arrived at the hospital, and Mother was still in the ER. There she met the orthopedic surgeon on call, who was very kind and compassionate. He offered the choice of surgery to fix the fracture, or palliative care in the form of opiates (narcotics) to keep her comfortable while nature took its course. Thinking it would give her superior pain relief, Ann opted for surgery. Mother was so confused she did not even know she had a broken hip!

When they transferred Mother to her hospital room, the nurses began getting her tucked in, taking blood pressure and pulse measurements, and they put a pulse oximeter on her finger. That device measured the degree of saturation of red blood cells with oxygen. Her first reading was lower than the 95 percent we like to see in medical practice.

Over the next few minutes the saturation dropped to the seventies, then to the sixties, and finally all the way down to 30 percent. At this point it was clear she was about to breathe her last. One of the nurses put her arm around Ann, whose face was now wet with tears. Another of the nurses was crying too. The charge nurse, who knew Ann had power of attorney and a Do Not Resuscitate order, asked her if she wanted them to put oxygen on Mother. Ann said, "No, let her go peacefully now so she won't have to go through the surgery."

They were all waiting quietly at her bedside when a brash young nurse rushed into the room with an oxygen mask. Ann said, "I'm her daughter. Mother doesn't want any heroic measures, and

I have medical power of attorney for her." The nurse replied curtly, "I don't know who you are!" She then shook Mother and slapped the mask onto her face. The saturation readings started to rise, and Mother started gasping and coughing and flailing her arms about.

The next afternoon she was sent to the operating room, and Ann went with her to communicate with the staff there. (Mother was totally deaf.) They sat in the pre-op waiting area for a very long time. Mother did not know who Ann was, and she could not carry on a conversation. All of a sudden she panicked, and said, "Oh, this is awful; I'm so scared!" She began pulling at her own arms, saying "why is everybody in *chains?*"

A few minutes passed, and her visage changed to one of pure delight. "Oh, this is so beautiful! You should see this. Everybody *loves* everyone here."

A nurse peeked around the curtain and said, "This is the strangest conversation I've ever heard." Ann guessed then that Mother had seen Hell—and Heaven.

When Mother woke up from the anesthesia in her hospital room, she began pulling at her catheter and her IV line. I spoke with her attending physician about sedating her. I told him Mother was extremely sensitive to drugs that had *anticholinergic* effects— she had once had an operation cancelled when an injection caused her heart to beat dangerously fast. I recommended one of the benzodiazepines instead.

The time came when Mother was stable enough for transfer to a rehabilitation facility. When the nurse came in to meet us, she said they would not be able to continue the Haldol the attending had given her for sedation. That was the exact drug I had tried to avoid; I was steamed! I felt her pulse and it was racing wildly and erratically.

The nursing home doctor started her on drugs to slow down the *tachycardia* and we waited, unsure what to do next. The next day the physical therapist took her to the exercise and gait training room to begin her rehabilitation. That continued for about three weeks, until Mother said she was too tired to do it any more. That meant her rehab stay was finished, and we would have to move her yet again, to a room upstairs. During that move, the social worker suggested we get hospice involved with her care.

We agreed, and she called Crossroads Hospice, who came quickly. They were exceedingly kind and compassionate, and they were very calming for Ann and for Mother. When we left for a while to buy supplies and move some furniture, a sitter came to stay with Mother while we were gone. The hospice workers relieved our exhaustion, and they were a big help to the nursing home staff as well.

Later that day Mother's breathing got more labored. The Crossroads nurse said they would give her some morphine to relieve her suffering. That worked wonders! She quit grasping for us, and began sleeping peacefully. It gave us just as much comfort, because her frantic reaching out to grab us had made us distraught.

The chaplain came and prayed with us and provided even more comfort for us. Easter came and went. Two days later the nurse called us at five o'clock in the morning to let us know Mother had died. We arrived a few minutes later and found they had put her favorite lipstick on her to embellish the permanent she had gotten a few days earlier. That gesture *really* touched our hearts. Ann and I rubbed Mother's arm and kissed her cheek. Hospice waited in the room with us until the funeral home arrived. We were comforted by the team that surrounded us.

The Hospice Movement

Over the next many months, we wondered out loud why we hadn't called hospice earlier. Our two-day experience with them satisfied us so much more than the two-month ordeal that had begun in the hospital ER. Ann, especially, had doubts about the way she had handled the whole painful experience. She encouraged me to visit with our local hospice, and to ask some questions that might give us closure on *our* performance in Mother's last weeks.

I made an appointment to spend some time with Dr. Jim Avery, Chief Executive Officer of Hospice of the Piedmont, the hospice serving our area in Virginia. The extraordinarily affable

Dr. Avery was so enthusiastic about hospice that we talked past our appointed time! He began by saying, "Hospice is intended for patients with a life expectancy of less than six months given the natural course of the disease and the expected treatment." When we had finished, I felt that I understood the goals and methods hospice uses, and it gave me confidence in their model of care at the end of life.

Dame Cicely Saunders founded the modern hospice movement in 1967. She served as the medical director of St. Christopher's Hospice in southwest London from that time until 1985. She died on July 14, 2005. A search of her name led me to an article announcing her death in The British Medical Journal.

The writer of the article, Caroline Richmond, said Doctor Saunders challenged the prevailing ethic—established through the *medicalization* of death—that not curing patients was a sign of failure. That ethic still today claims that it is desirable to lie to people about their prognosis. In its place, Dr. Saunders introduced effective pain management and insisted that dying people need dignity, compassion, and respect along with science.

She introduced the concept of "total pain," which included the physical, emotional, social, and spiritual dimensions of distress. She rejected the notion that *dying* people should wait until their pain killers had worn off before receiving another dose. To her, the risk of opiate addiction held no sway in their pain management. Her work has endured because experience tells us that death is not usually a *medical* event.

Most people die gradually, Dr. Avery says, through an orderly and natural series of physical changes, which are not medical emergencies requiring intervention. He stresses that an interdisciplinary team is best qualified to achieve the goals of managing "total pain."

Physicians and nurses manage physical pain. Social workers lead the effort to assuage social and psychological pain. They must address financial troubles, family conflicts, depression, anxiety, deep wounds from the past, and harm done by the patient to other people. Chaplains guide the patients and their families through the spiritual distress that often accompanies dying. They frequently encounter guilt, doubt, the burden of sins, terror of the afterlife, and lack of connection to a higher power.

Dr. Avery tells the nursing and medical students at the University of Virginia that the "h" in hospice stands for Hope. Using validated scales of measurement, he shows them how hope declines until week two, and then goes up and up. Identifying three stages of hope in the dying patient, hospice leads patients through the hope for a cure, to the hope for prolonging life, and on to the final stage—the hopes of the dying.

The hopes of most dying people include the hope of giving and receiving love. The hope of being physically comfortable and of not being alone follows closely on the heels of the hope for love. Finally, the hope of *reconciliation* through forgiving and being forgiven stands high on the list of hopes of the dying.

The hope therapy that hospice offers also addresses spiritual hopes—hope that one is accomplishing God's plan, that one's life has meaning and purpose, that one is "saved," and that one will see one's family and the Savior in Heaven. The chaplains are a busy bunch!

If you doubt that hope is really all that important, consider the following: an article in the Journal of the American Medical Association in 1977 (volume 27:1720) reveals that *hopelessness* is the number one reason patients request physician-assisted suicide in the Netherlands. Only 5 percent of them say that pain is the reason for their request.

Hospice Use Varies a Lot

The Dartmouth Atlas of Health Care examines American attitudes about death and dying. It is one of the "key issues" on their website; they have this to say about their findings:

> "What do patients want at the end of life? Do they want their physicians to do everything possible to extend life? Do they want more time in the hospital? If additional treatments offer little possibility of benefit, do they want

more invasive care? Research suggests that the care they get is not necessarily the care they want. Evidence comes from a large-scale study funded by the Robert Wood Johnson Foundation. Most patients with serious illness said they would prefer to die at home. Yet most patients died in the hospitals, and care was rarely aligned with their reported preferences, even though extensive efforts were made by trained nurses to align their care with their wishes. For example, among the patients who indicated that they preferred to die at home, the majority—55 percent—actually died in the hospital. The evidence therefore suggests that patients often prefer a more conservative pattern of end-of-life care than they actually receive—and that a patient's wishes can be less influential than the practice patterns at the hospital where care is delivered."

The Dartmouth researchers find that the percent of deaths occurring *in hospital* in 2010 varies from a high of 41 percent in New York to a low of 16 percent in Utah. If the residents of New York use hospice as often as the residents of states like Utah, as many as 12,000 percent *fewer* New Yorkers will die in a hospital!

The National Hospice and Palliative Care Organization's 2013 report shows that the number of hospice providers is growing steadily. But in spite of a concomitant increase in the number of patients served, the use of hospice remains spotty in the United States.

People living in Utah and Arizona spend more than one and one-half (1.5) times as many days in hospice care in the last six months of life as the average American. Alabama and South Carolina have ratios to the national average of 1.36 and 1.29, respectively. On the other hand, New Yorkers average only eleven days per decedent—just one-half the national rate. If they use hospice at just the *average rate*, they will spend 645,172 more days in hospice care in a year. (The Dartmouth Atlas, 2010)

Even within New York, however, the pattern is not uniform. Dartmouth's work shows a two-fold variation among the state's ten hospital regions. The following table shows the population, the average days/decedent (rate), the ratio to the state average, and the number of days in each region, above or below the number predicted by the statewide experience. For brevity's sake, I abbreviate the table to show only the regions with the highest and lowest rates.

Region	Population	Rate	Ratio to State	Surplus/Deficit
New York State	64,410	11.0		
Albany	8,393	15.1	1.37	+34,037
Buffalo	4,118	13.4	1.22	+9,928
East Long Island	16,466	10.6	0.97	-5,981
Syracuse	5,082	7.6	0.69	-17,328
Elmira	1,868	7.5	0.68	-6,646

The regions at the bottom of the table—those using a lower number of hospice days—also have, as you might expect, a higher percentage of deaths occurring in hospital. In fact, the people in East Long Island suffer the second highest rate of in hospital deaths (36 percent) in the nation—far above the national average of 24 percent. (data from 2010)

Our personal experience, recounted at the beginning of this chapter, was very painful. We are grateful for the comfort hospice provided at the end. I hope and pray that your local hospice providers will make your task easier when you are faced with the death of someone near and dear to you. It is a real life alternative to a high tech death—hooked up to machines and alone—in a hospital ICU.

I know, however, that careful planning, constant praying, and conscientious performance will not guarantee the results you desire. So don't freak out if everything doesn't fall into place the way you want it to. I remember an elderly couple in our neighborhood. His wife was terminally ill, and he sat by her bedside day after day, waiting for the Lord to take her home. Finally, after several sleepless nights and days, he decided to go home to bathe and get some rest. While he was gone, she died. It didn't seem fair!

When we hear stories like that, we simply cannot make sense of it. We can only humble ourselves under the hand of God—our

Creator. Our neighbor's wife might have needed that time alone with the Lord. Jesus says, "Are not two sparrows sold for a penny? And not one of them will fall to the ground apart from your Father. But even the hairs of your head are all numbered" (Matthew 10: 29–30). He also says, "In the world you will have tribulation. But take heart; I have overcome the world" (John 16:33). When the world throws the worst it has at us, we can still cling to Christ.

In a letter to the first church he established on European soil, Paul says, "The Lord is at hand; do not be anxious about anything, but in everything by prayer and supplication with thanksgiving let your requests be made known to God. And the peace of God . . . will guard your hearts and your minds in Christ Jesus" (Philippians 4: 5b–7).

We know that the one who raised Jesus from the dead will also raise us to be with him. "So we do not lose heart. Though our outer self is wasting away, our inner self is being renewed day by day. For this light momentary affliction is preparing for us an eternal weight of glory beyond all comparison" (Second Corinthians 4: 16–17).

Jesus loves us! He revealed to his disciple John that he was going away to prepare a place for us in advance of our joining him. John described it this way:

> "And I saw the holy city, new Jerusalem, coming down out of heaven from God, prepared as a bride adorned for her husband. And I heard a loud voice from the throne saying, 'Behold, the dwelling place of God is with man. He will dwell with them, and they will be his people, and God himself will be with them as their God. He will wipe away every tear from their eyes, and death shall be no more, neither shall there be mourning, nor crying, nor pain anymore, for the former things have passed away'" (Revelation 21: 2–4).